NEW JERSEY'S FIRST SUPERHERO

THE TOXIC AVENGER MUSICAL

Book & Lyrics by **Joe DiPietro** Music & Lyrics by **David Bryan**
Based on Lloyd Kaufman's The Toxic Avenger
Presented by **Jean Cheever** and **Tom Polum**
with
Sara Chase   Nick Cordero   Demond Green   Matthew Saldivar
and
Nancy Opel

Scenic Design	Costume Design	Lighting Design	Sound Design
Beowulf Boritt	**David C. Woolard**	**Kenneth Posner**	**Kurt Fischer**

Hair & Make-Up Design
Mark Adam Rampmeyer

Prosthetics & Special Effects Design
John Dods

Fight Direction
Rick Sordelet & David DeBesse

Casting
McCorkle Casting

Production Management
Robert G. Mahon III & Jeff Wild

Production Stage Manager
Scott Taylor Rollison

Advertising & Marketing
Allied Live, LLC

Logo Design & Graphics
**The Bradford Lawton
Design Group**

NJ Marketing
Kelly Ryman

Press Representation
O & M Co.

Audience Development
Meri Krassner

Company Manager
Megan Trice

Music Direction
Doug Katsaros

Orchestrations & Arrangements
**David Bryan
& Christopher Jahnke**

General Management
**Splinter Group
Productions**

Choreographed by
Wendy Seyb
Directed by **John Rando**

2009 Cast Recording Available from Time Life

The producers wish to express their appreciation to Theatre Development Fund for its support of this production.

World Premiere Production Presented by George Street Playhouse, October 10, 2008
David Saint, Artistic Director Todd Schmidt, Managing Director

ISBN 978-1-4234-9483-6

HAL•LEONARD®
CORPORATION
7777 W. BLUEMOUND RD. P.O. BOX 13819 MILWAUKEE, WI 53213

In Australia Contact:
Hal Leonard Australia Pty. Ltd.
4 Lentara Court
Cheltenham, Victoria, 3192 Australia
Email: ausadmin@halleonard.com.au

Visit Hal Leonard Online at
www.halleonard.com

4   WHO WILL SAVE NEW JERSEY?

18   JERSEY GIRL

24   MY BIG FRENCH BOYFRIEND

31   THANK GOD SHE'S BLIND

37   BIG GREEN FREAK

44   CHOOSE ME, OPRAH!

54   HOT TOXIC LOVE

62   THE LEGEND OF THE TOXIC AVENGER

67   EVIL IS HOT

71   BITCH/SLUT/LIAR/WHORE

76   YOU TORE MY HEART OUT

81   ALL MEN ARE FREAKS

87   A BRAND NEW DAY IN NEW JERSEY

WHO WILL SAVE NEW JERSEY?

Music by DAVID BRYAN
Lyrics by JOE DiPIETRO
and DAVID BRYAN

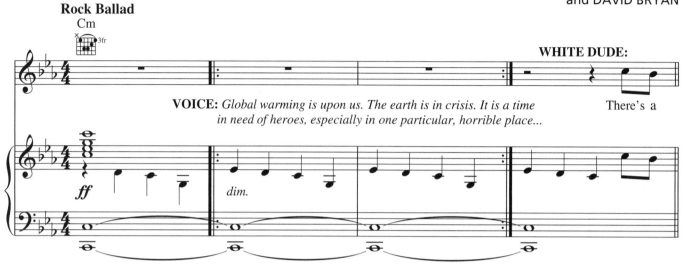

VOICE: *Global warming is upon us. The earth is in crisis. It is a time in need of heroes, especially in one particular, horrible place...*

WHITE DUDE:
There's a

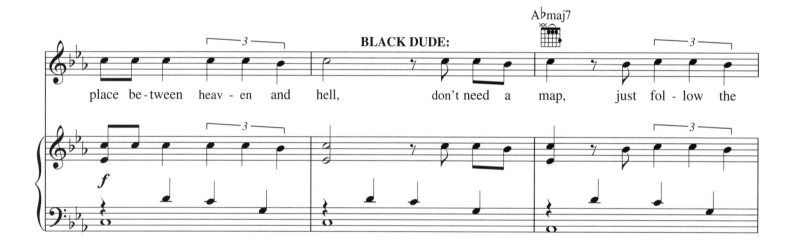

place be-tween heav - en and hell, **BLACK DUDE:** don't need a map, just fol - low the

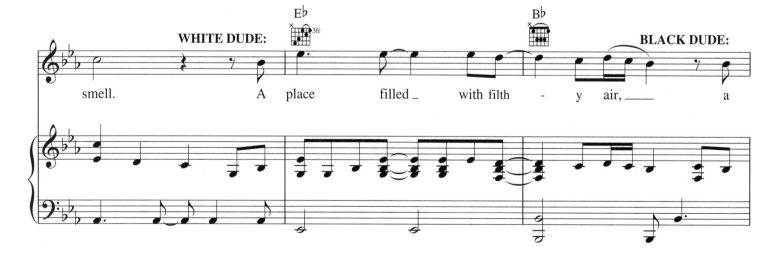

smell. **WHITE DUDE:** A place filled _ with filth - y air, _ **BLACK DUDE:** a

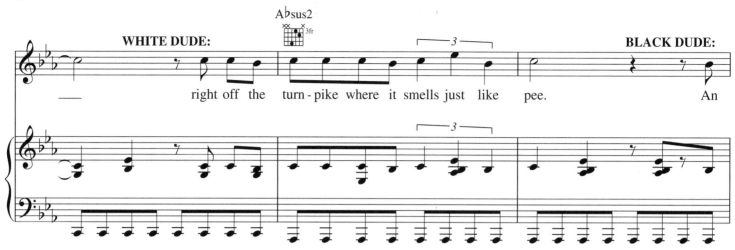

WHITE DUDE: right off the turn-pike where it smells just like pee.

BLACK DUDE: An

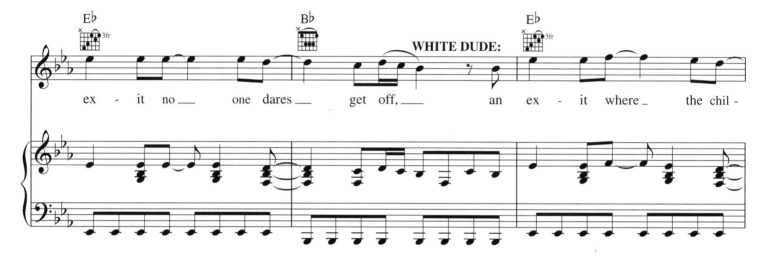

WHITE DUDE: ex - it no __ one dares __ get off, __ an ex - it where __ the chil -

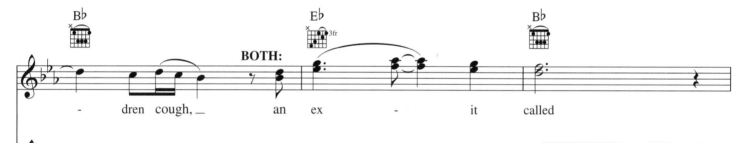

BOTH: - dren cough, __ an ex - it called

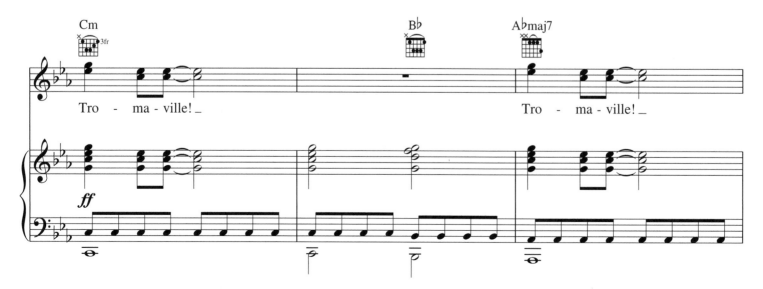

Tro - ma - ville! __ Tro - ma - ville! __

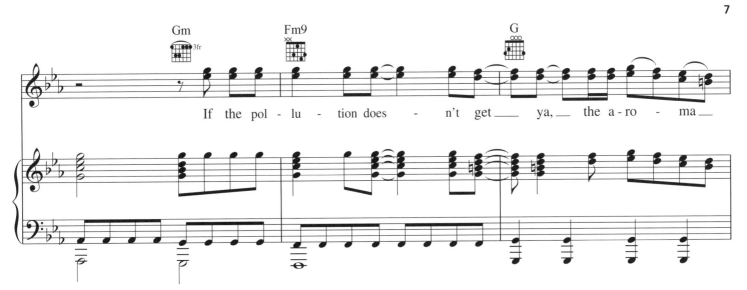

If the pol - lu - tion does - n't get___ ya,___ the a - ro - ma___

will!

NUN:

Who will save New

Jer - sey? We're dy - ing for some air. There's

no hope in New Jer - sey, Lord.___ Does an - y - bod - y care?___

8

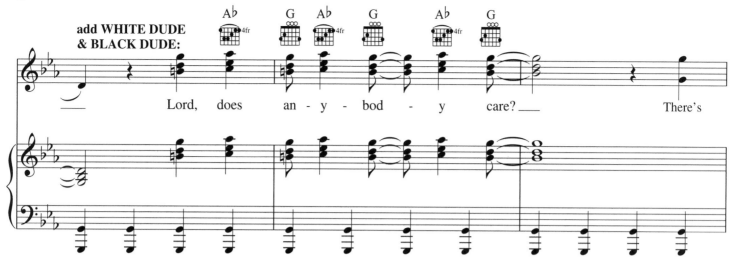

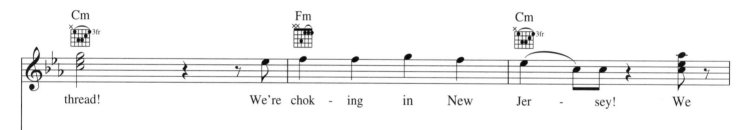

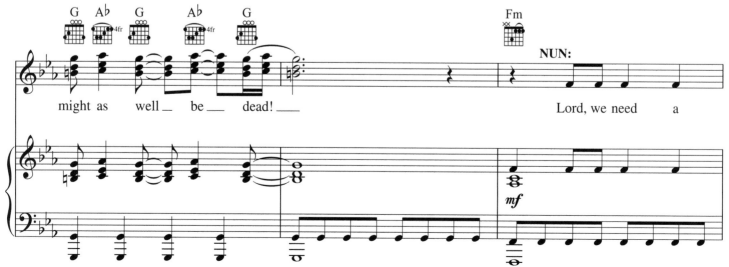

fa - vor. ___ We need a sav - vy sav - ior. ___ But

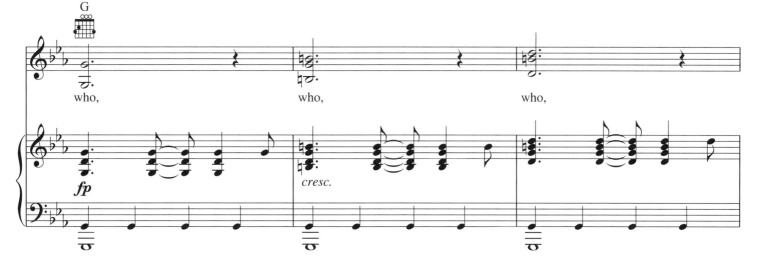

who, who, who,

who? **MELVIN:** I will save New Jer - sey! ___ I'm

Mel - vin Ferd, _ the Third. _____ I'm here for you, _ New Jer -

NUN: *Not him, Lord!*

-sey, — on that you have — my _____ word.

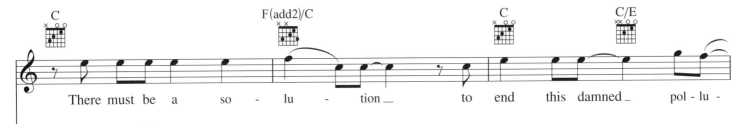

There must be a so - lu - tion — to end this damned — pol - lu-

-tion. — It's time to start — a glo - bal rev - o-

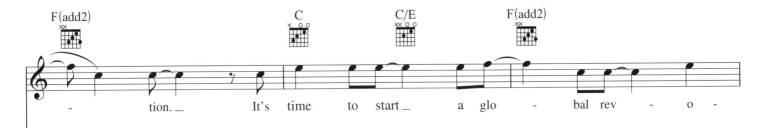

lu - - - tion! _____ MELVIN: *Sister, look at what has infested our town!*

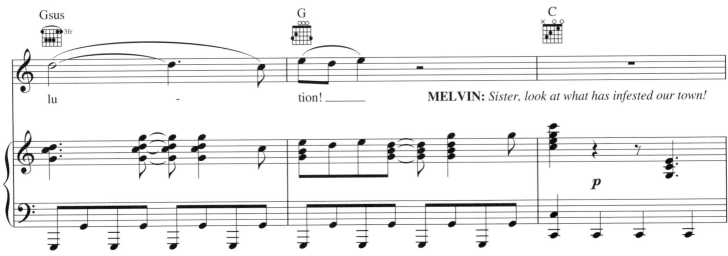

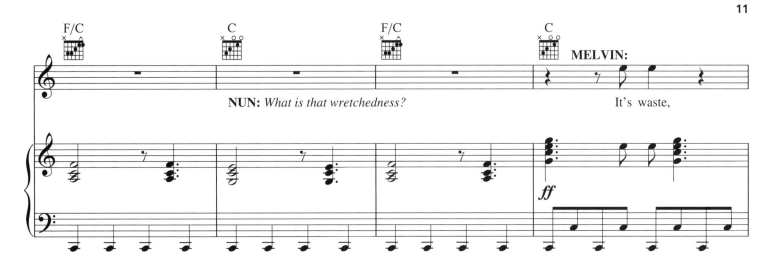

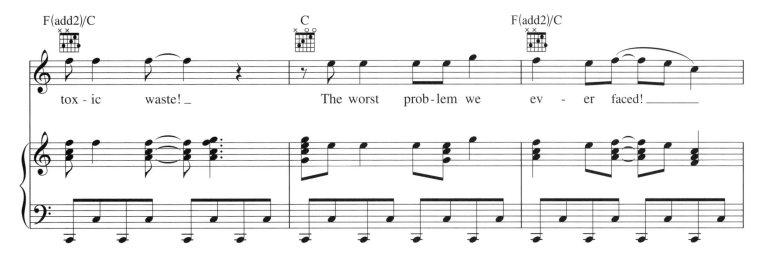

NUN:

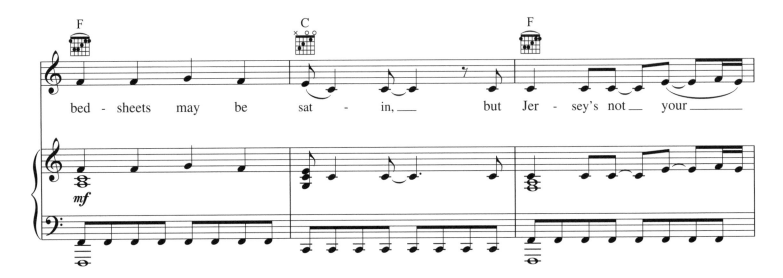

add MELVIN:

L'istesso tempo

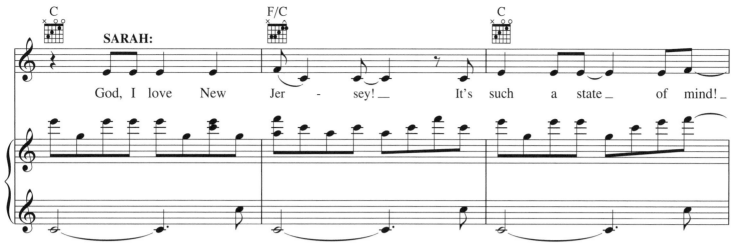

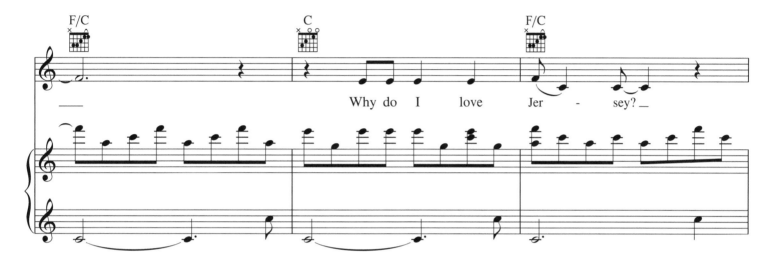

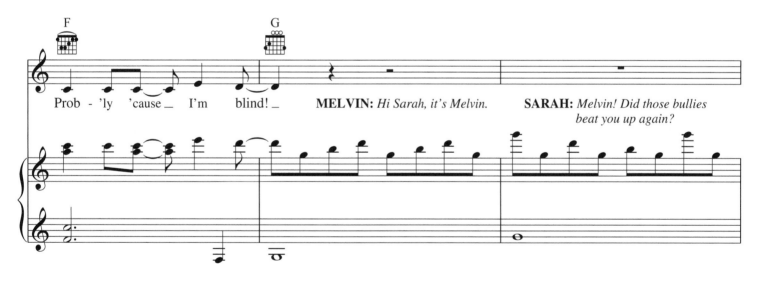

14

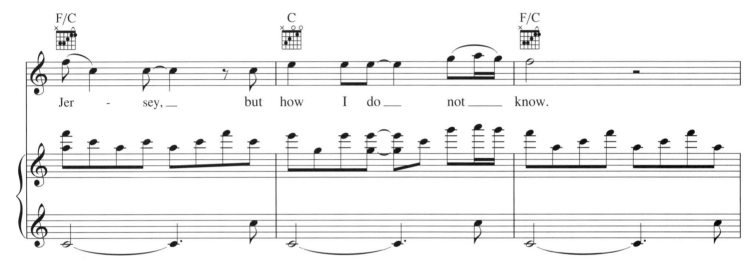

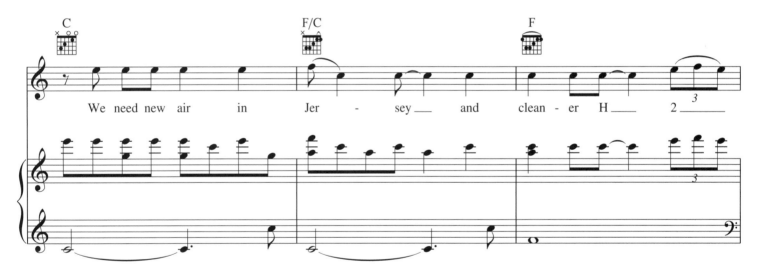

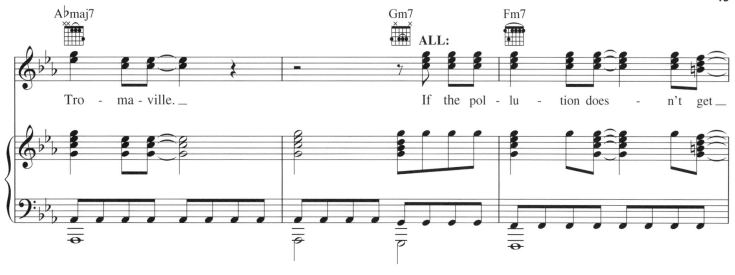

Tro - ma - ville. ___ If the pol - lu - tion does - n't get ___

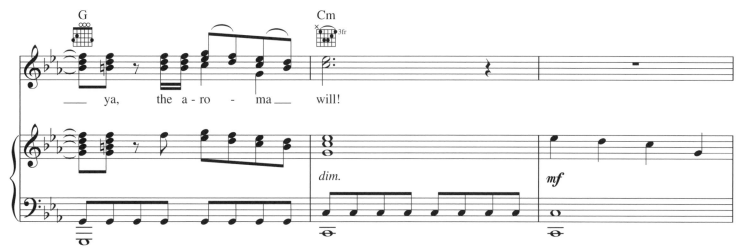

___ ya, the a - ro - ma ___ will!

dim. *mf*

WHITE DUDE: *So there you have it. There will be no intermission tonight.*

The show is eight hours long.

ALL:

Help us, we're New

cresc. *ff*

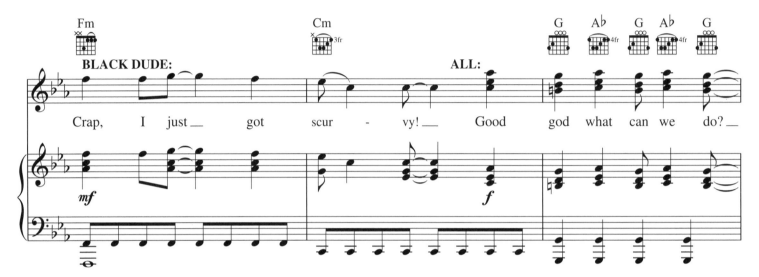

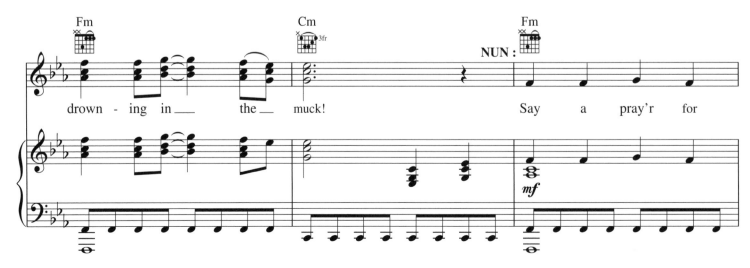

JERSEY GIRL

Music by DAVID BRYAN
Lyrics by JOE DiPIETRO
and DAVID BRYAN

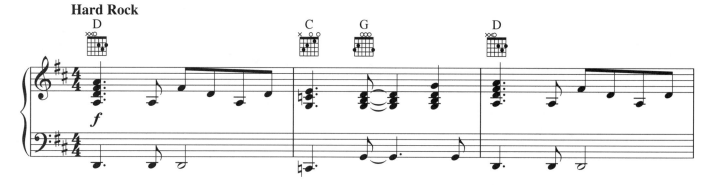

MAYOR:

I'm the may - or of this crap - py town, __

so let me tell you how it's gon - na go down. __ I'm gon - na store your __

tox - ic trash ___ and you will pay me boat - loads of

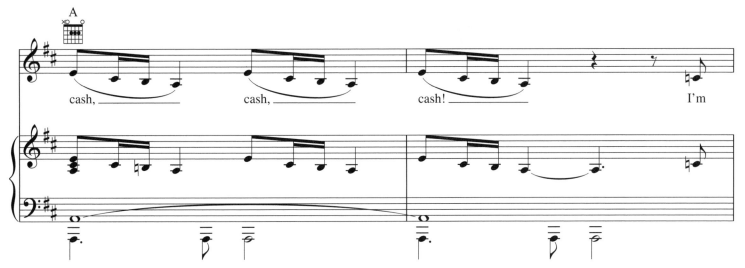

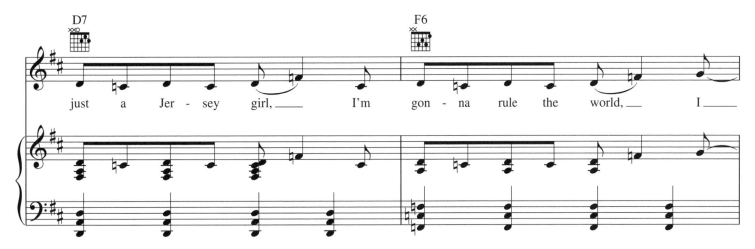

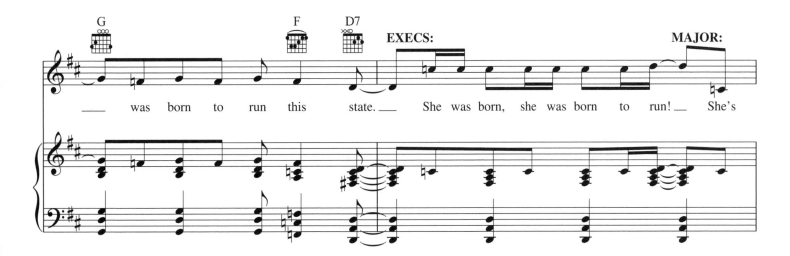

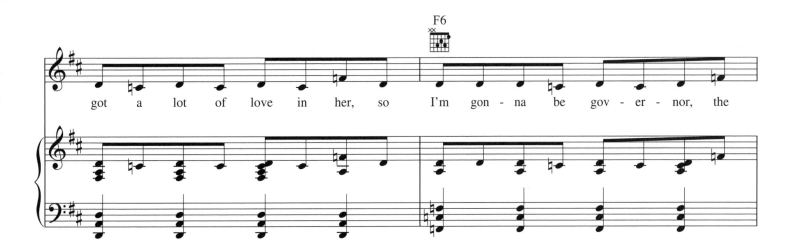

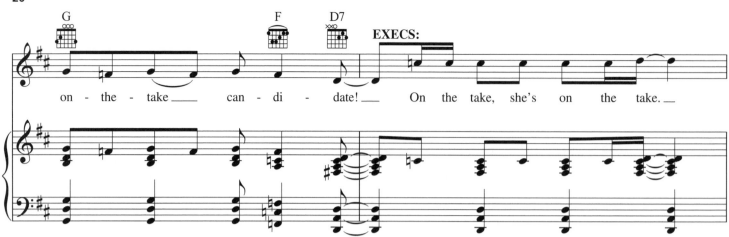

on - the - take ___ can - di - date! ___ On the take, she's on the take. ___

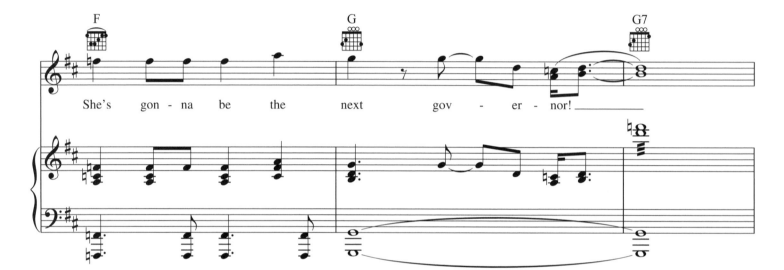

She's gon - na be the next gov - er - nor! _____

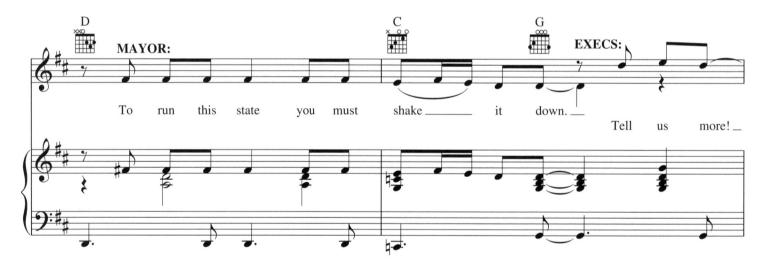

MAYOR: To run this state you must shake _____ it down. __ EXECS: Tell us more! __

MAYOR: ___ You'll lie or cheat __ or ____ sleep _____ a - round. __ EXECS: She's a whore! __

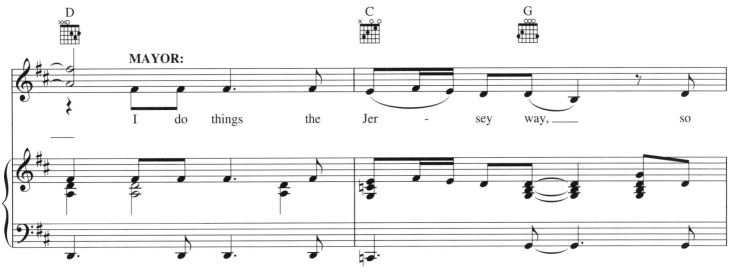

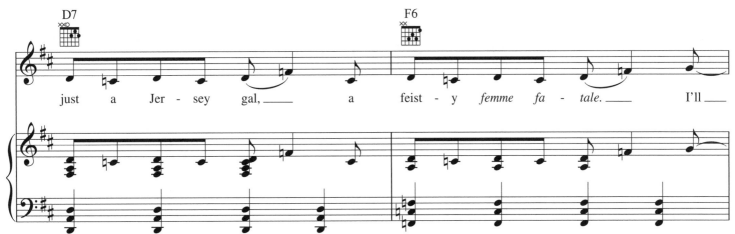

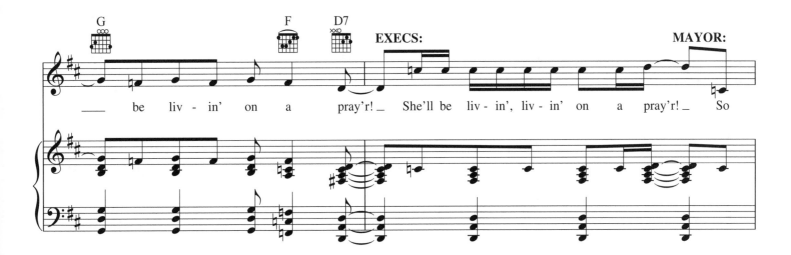

watch me as I cam-paign through snow and sleet and ac-id rain. Can you

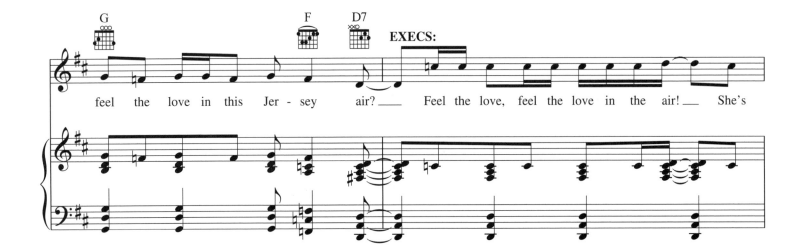

feel the love in this Jer-sey air? __ Feel the love, feel the love in the air! __ She's

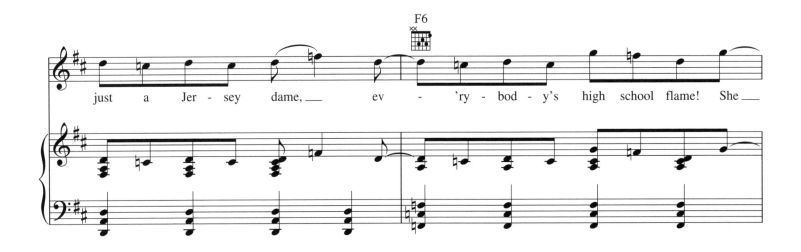

just a Jer-sey dame, __ ev-'ry-bod-y's high school flame! She __

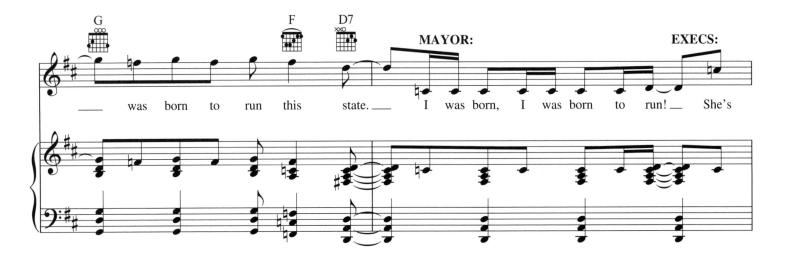

was born to run this state. __ I was born, I was born to run! __ She's

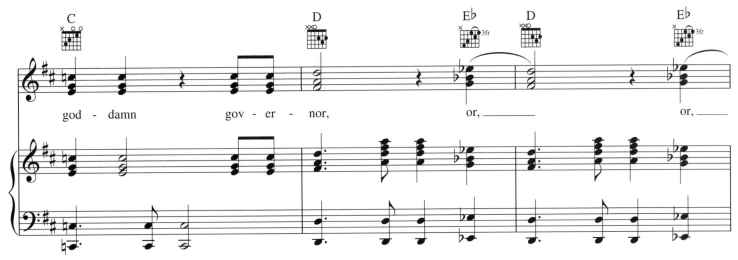

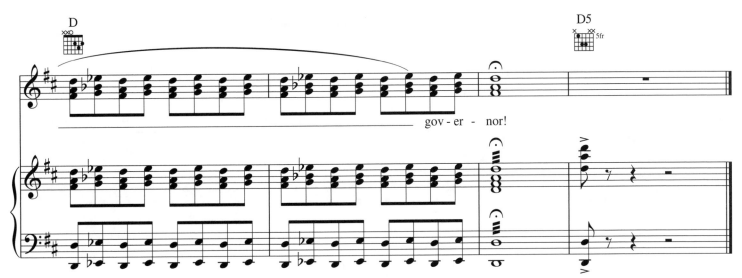

MY BIG FRENCH BOYFRIEND

Music by DAVID BRYAN
Lyrics by JOE DiPIETRO
and DAVID BRYAN

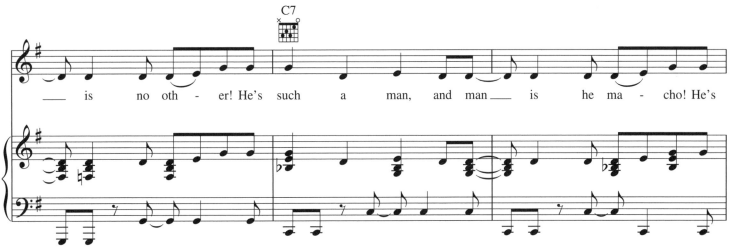

is no oth - er! He's such a man, and man __ is he ma - cho! He's

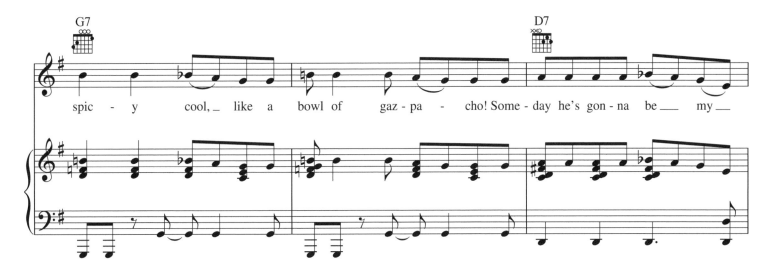

spic - y cool, __ like a bowl of gaz - pa - cho! Some - day he's gon - na be __ my __

big, my big French boy - friend. *I've got to call my best friends in the whole world!*

Hey, Shin - e - qua, I ___ met this fly __ man!

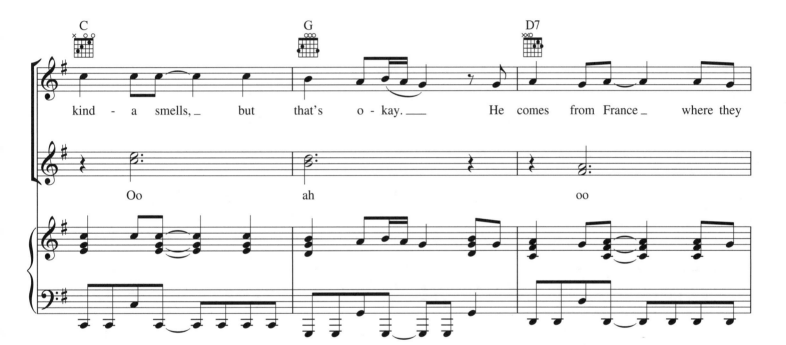

love this guy! He sounds real - ly hunk - y. His chest is huge! He's __

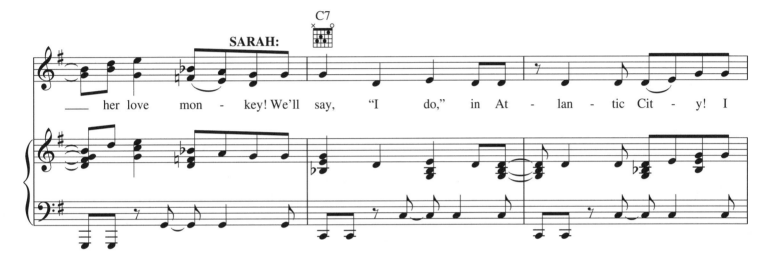

__ her love mon - key! We'll say, "I do," in At - lan - tic Cit - y! I

bet our kids are gon - na be pret - ty! I don't e - ven mind __ the __

stench! He's French! He's a he - ro, he's a sav - ior, he's a mensch! I'm ver - klempt! I'll

be his ev-er lov-ing___ wench! He's my big French boy-friend!

SHINEQUA & DIANE:

Her big French boy-

My big French boy-friend!

friend! ___

Her B F B F. ___

rit.

Freely

ad lib. N.C. **ALL:**

My, ___ my big French boy-friend!

a tempo

THANK GOD SHE'S BLIND

Music by DAVID BRYAN
Lyrics by JOE DiPIETRO
and DAVID BRYAN

Big Rock Ballad

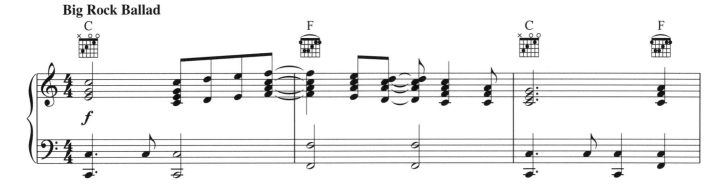

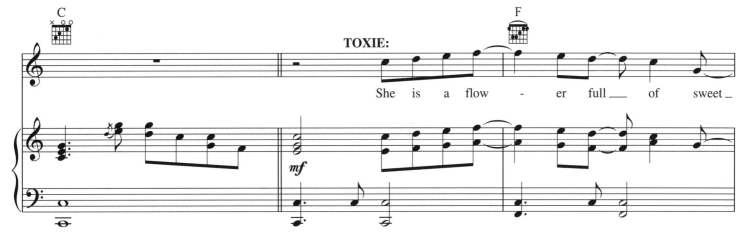

TOXIE:
She is a flow - er full __ of sweet __ per - fume. She steals my breath __

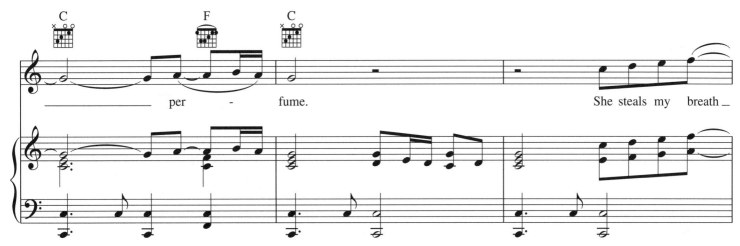

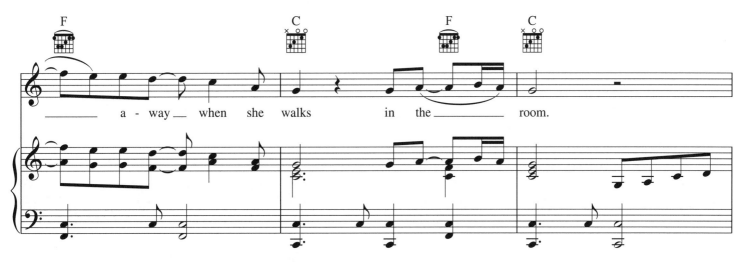

__ a - way __ when she walks in the __ room.

A wom-an like that _____ is so _____ hard _____ to find. _____

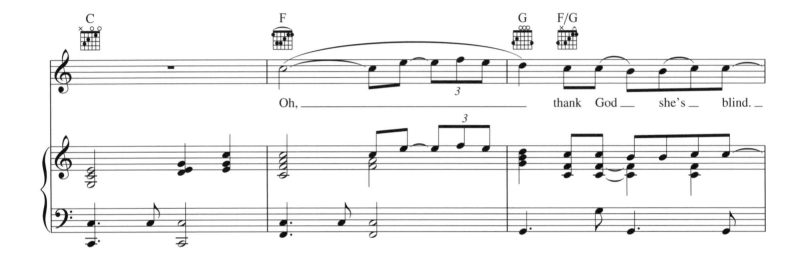

Oh, _____ thank God _____ she's _____ blind. _____

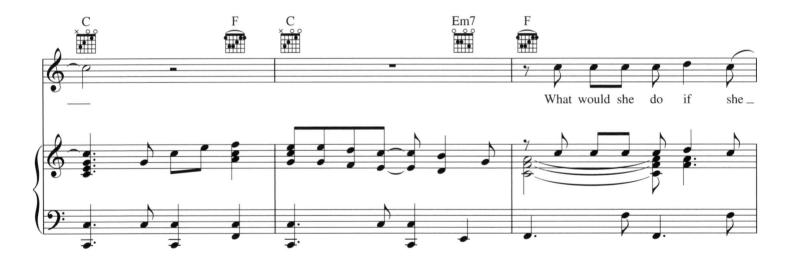

What would she do if she _____

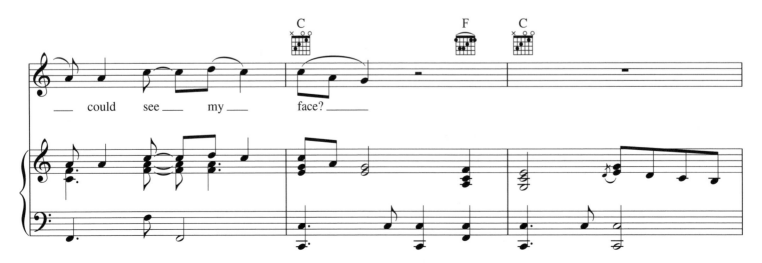

_____ could see _____ my _____ face? _____

Would she love it ten - der or _____ spray ____ it ____ full ____ of mace? __

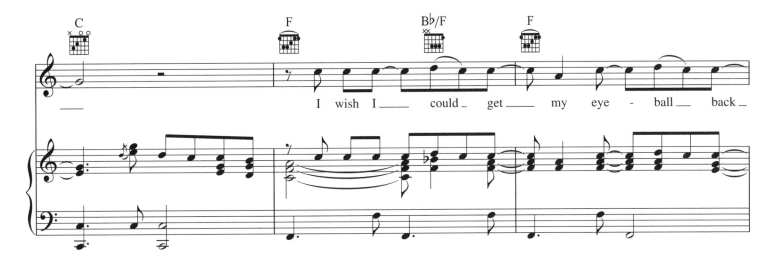

I wish I ____ could ____ get ____ my eye - ball ____ back ____

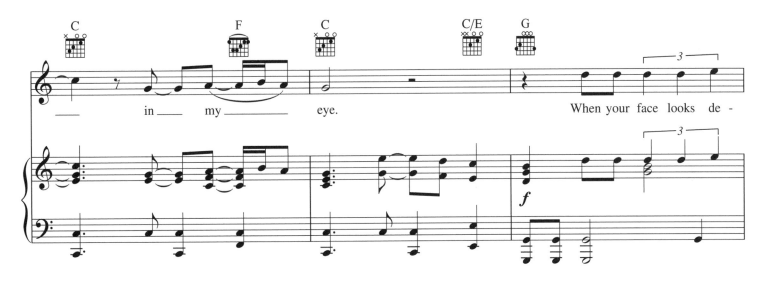

in ____ my _____ eye. When your face looks de -

cayed, _____ it's hard to get laid. _____

But she thinks I'm one _____ beau - ti - ful guy!

I _____ will give _____ her _____ this ge - ra - ni -

um _____ and pray that she does - n't touch my cra -

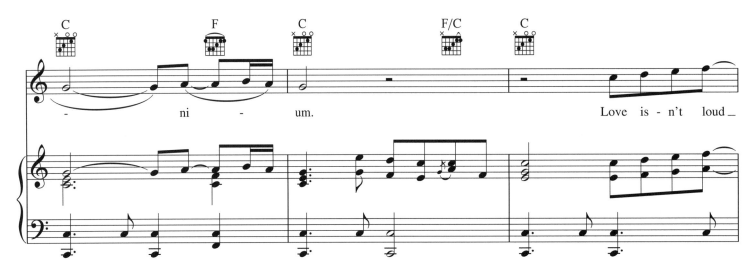

- ni - um. Love is - n't loud _____

at all, ___ it's soft ___ and kind. ___

Oh, _____ thank God __ she's _ blind. ___

Oh, _____ thank God __ she's _ blind. ___

I see that hand, I see that guy! I

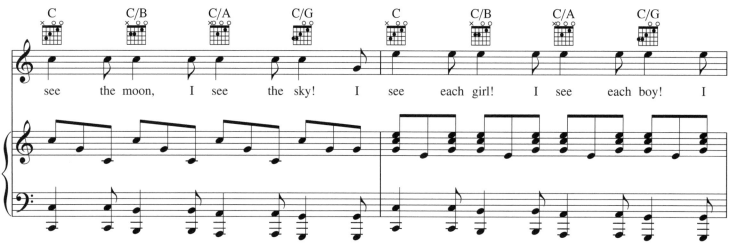

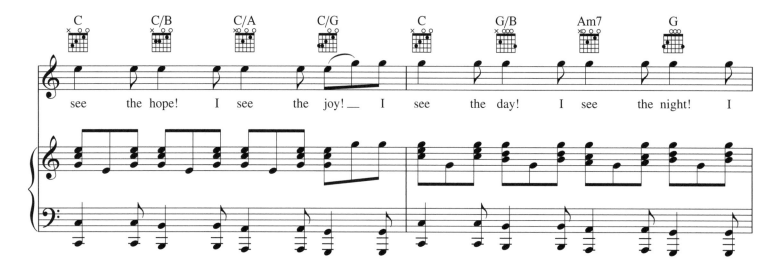

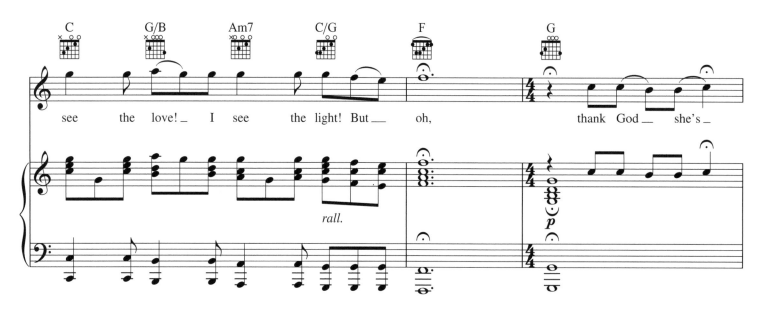

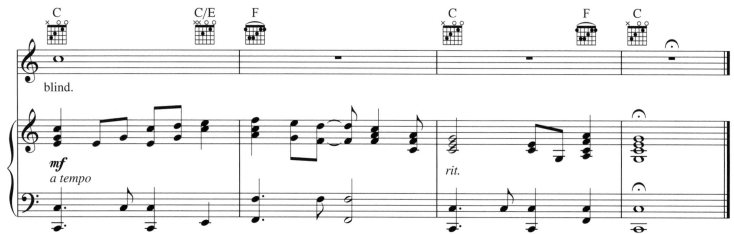

BIG GREEN FREAK

Music by DAVID BRYAN
Lyrics by JOE DiPIETRO
and DAVID BRYAN

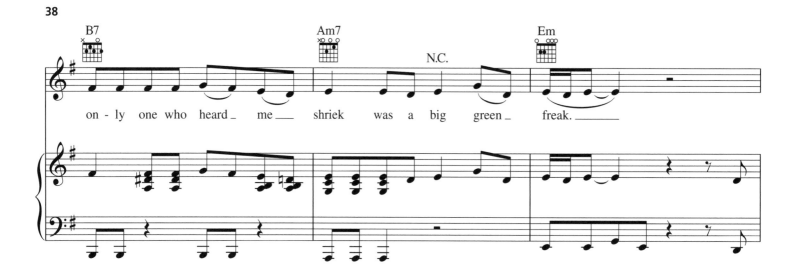

on - ly one who heard _ me _ shriek was a big green _ freak. _

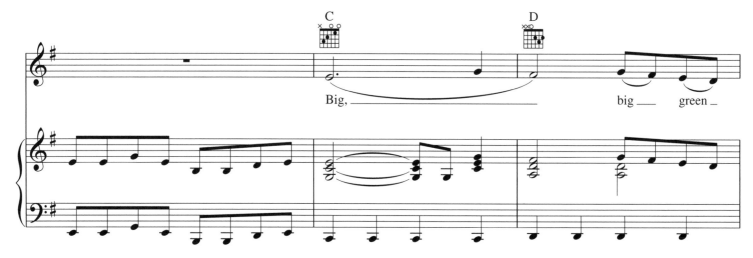

Big, _____ big _ green _

DR. FISHBEIN:

freak! I've done ev-'ry test that ex - ists. _

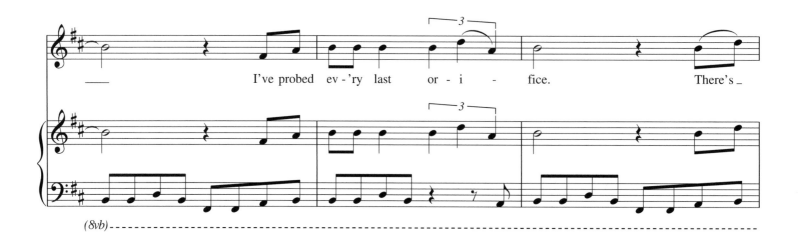

I've probed ev-'ry last or - i - fice. There's _

on - ly one thing that I know: This _ ain't cov-ered by your H M

O. _____ And my di - ag - no - sis is _ u - nique, you're a big green _

freak. ___ Big, _____

_ big _ green _ freak!

MAYOR:

Tro-ma-ville's in trou-ble, there's a mon-ster in town. _ Wel-come to New Jer-sey, we'll nail your

balls to the ground. _ Your mon-ster reign of ter - ror will come to an end! __ Your

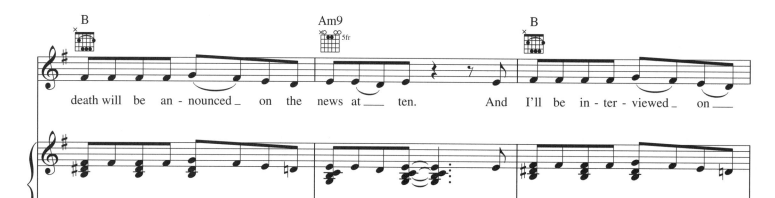

death will be an-nounced _ on the news at __ ten. And I'll be in - ter - viewed _ on __

PROFESSOR KEN:

C N __ N! __ Yeah, _ C N N! __   Well, the

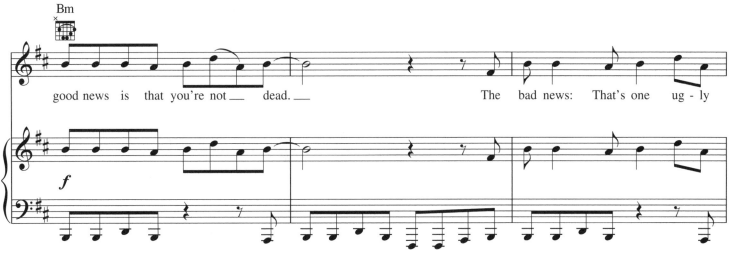

good news is that you're not __ dead. __ The bad news: That's one ug - ly

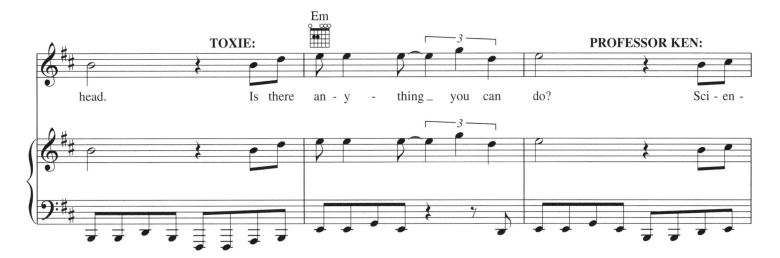

TOXIE: **PROFESSOR KEN:**

head. Is there an - y - thing __ you can do? Sci - en -

tif - i - cal - ly speak-ing, you're screwed. __ Hey, at least you got a real __ nice phy -

sique for a big green __ freak!

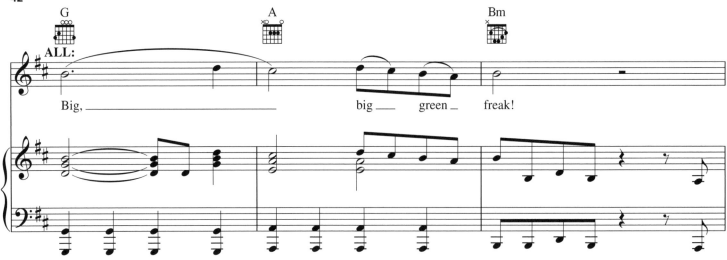

Big, _____ big __ green __ freak!

Slowly

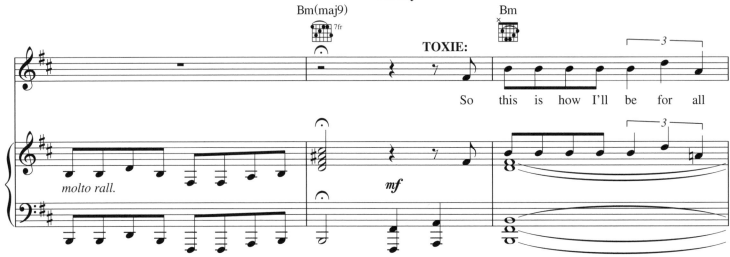

So this is how I'll be for all

molto rall.

time, a freak of na - ture ooz - ing slime. _____ I

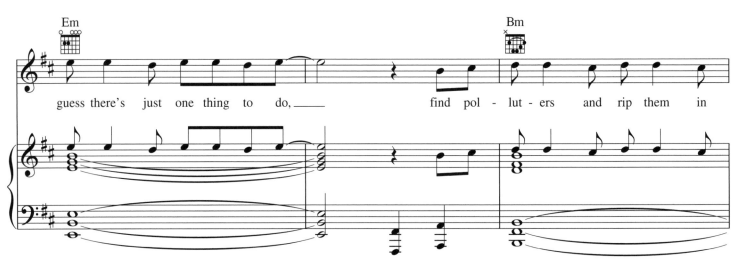

guess there's just one thing to do, _____ find pol - lut - ers and rip them in

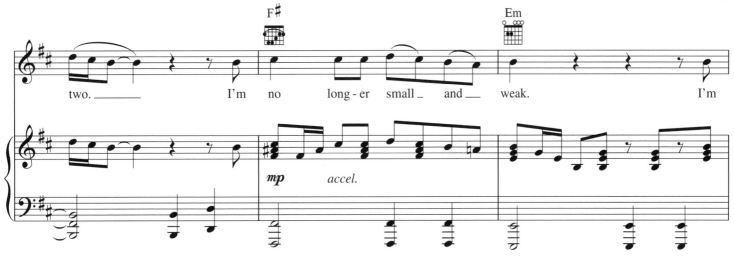

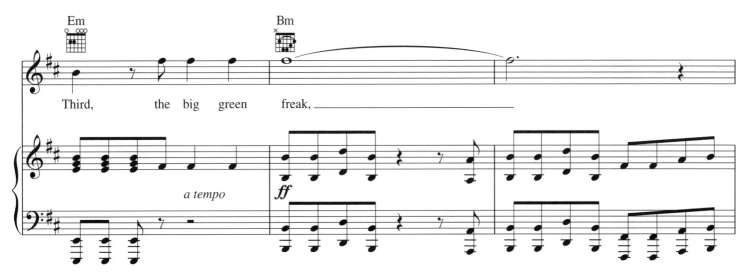

CHOOSE ME, OPRAH!

Music by DAVID BRYAN
Lyrics by JOE DiPIETRO
and DAVID BRYAN

Pronounced "thee"

Choose me, O - prah! Use me, O - prah!

Make me a per - son peo - ple a - dore! _____ Hug me, O - prah!

Plug me, O - prah! I'll be your book-sell - ing ___ whore!

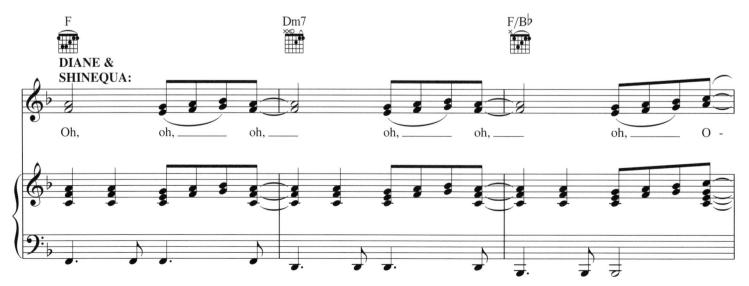

DIANE & SHINEQUA:

Oh, oh, _____ oh, _____ oh, _____ oh, _____ oh, _____ O -

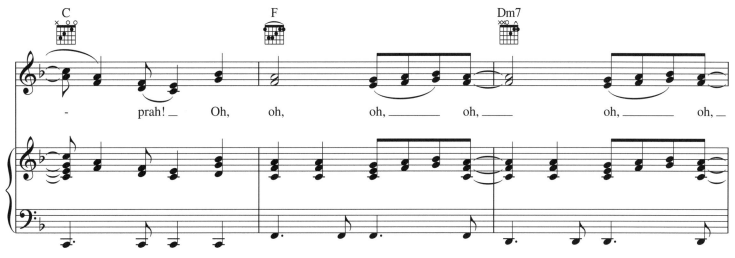

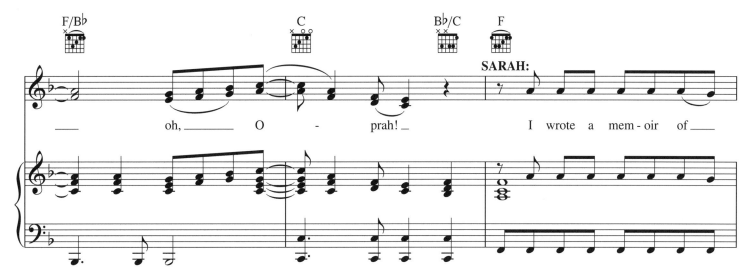

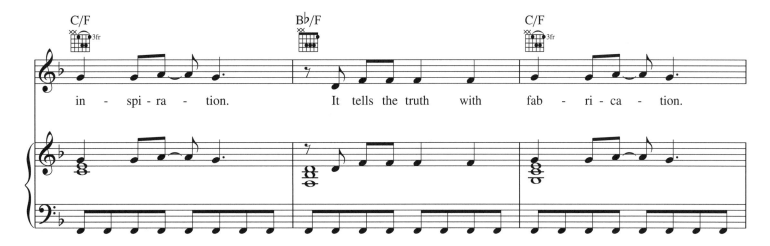

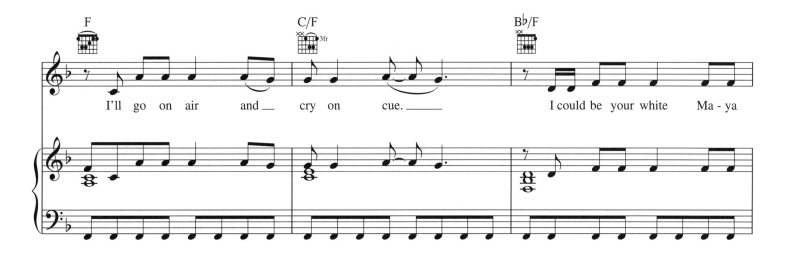

An-ge-lou! _____ My tome is a tale of a wom-an in charge.

DIANE & SHINEQUA:

An-ge-lou! _____

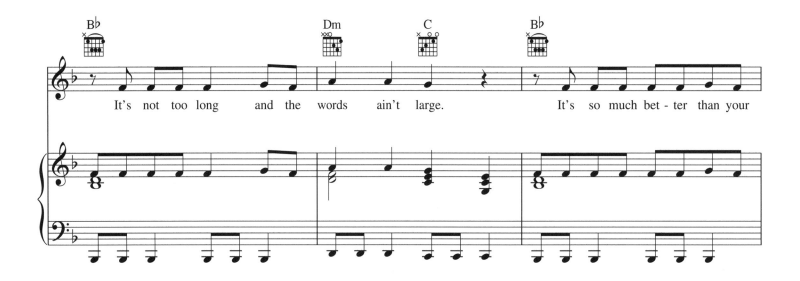

It's not too long and the words ain't large. It's so much bet-ter than your

u-su-al crap, and I got a mar-ket-a-ble hand-i-cap! _____

49

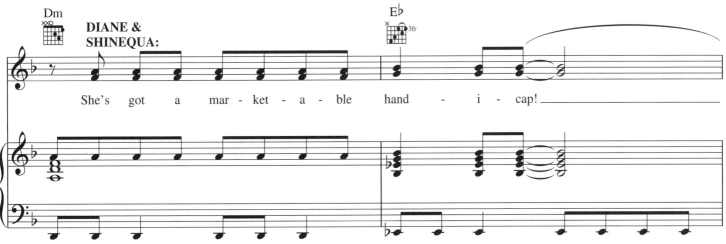

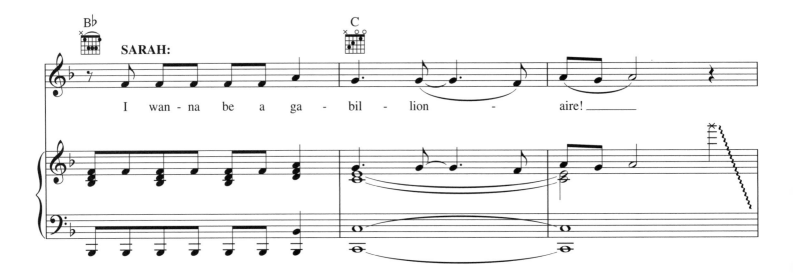

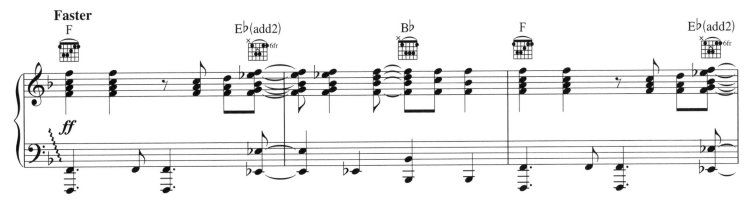

I said, O - prah! Sell - ing more ___ and more. ___

I said, O - prah! I said,

I'll be your book ___ sell - ing whore! ___ Bet - ter than u -

O - prah! I said, O - prah!

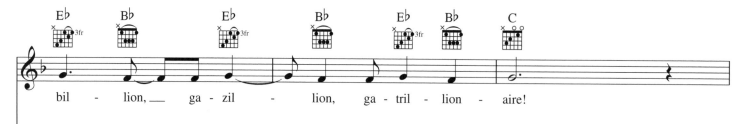

HOT TOXIC LOVE

Music by DAVID BRYAN
Lyrics by JOE DiPIETRO
and DAVID BRYAN

Moderately slow Rock Ballad, in 1

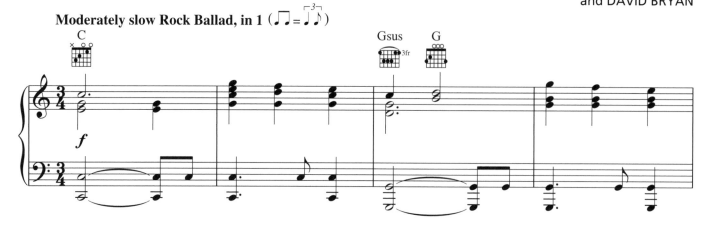

TOXIE:
I al - ways dreamed ___ I'd find ___ some - one, ___ but

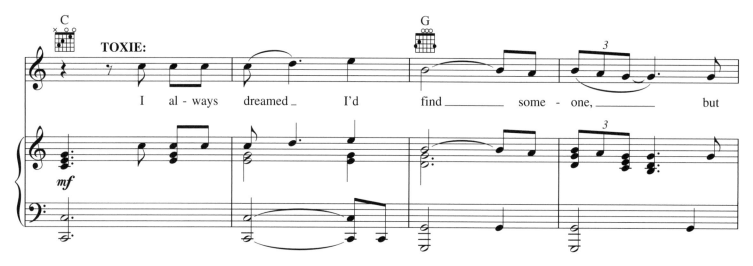

that was just some fan - ta - sy. ___

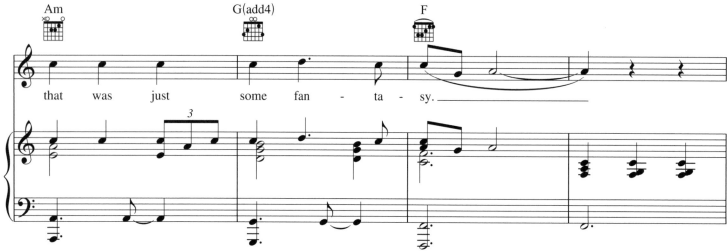

I'd meet a girl and she'd _____ up and run. _____

Love want - ed no part of me. _____

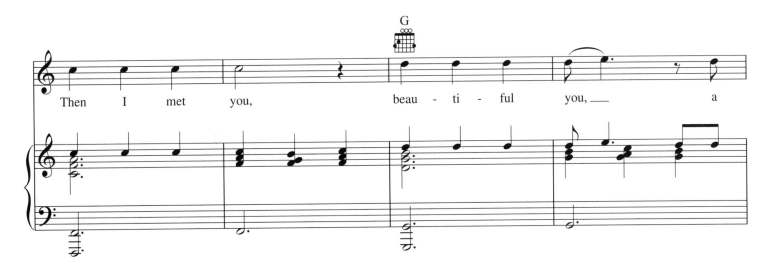

Then I met you, beau - ti - ful you, _____ a

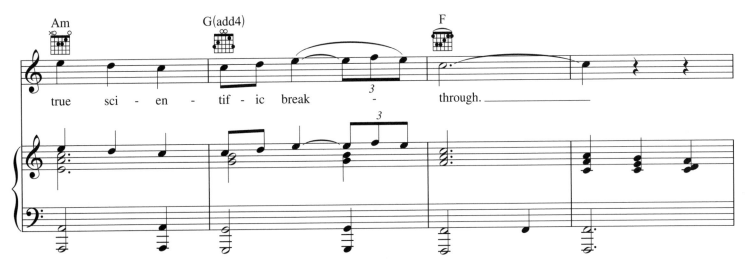

true sci - en - tif - ic break - through. _____

Look deep in - side, _____ I have noth - ing to hide. You _____

see the real me, I'm yours hon - est - ly. _____ You

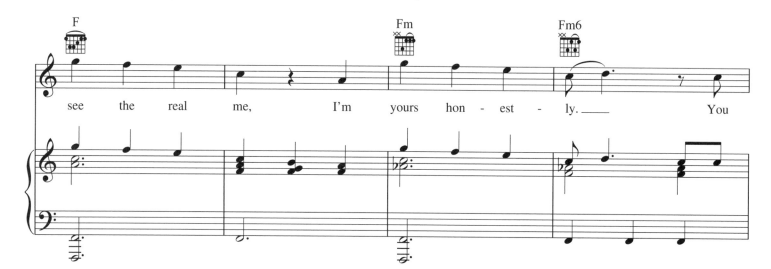

make me com - bust _____ with chem - i - cal lust. I'm _____

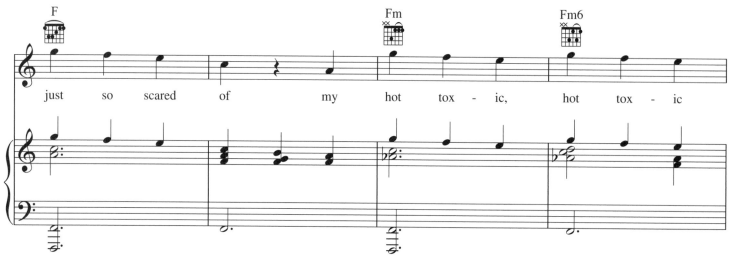

just so scared of my hot tox - ic, hot tox - ic

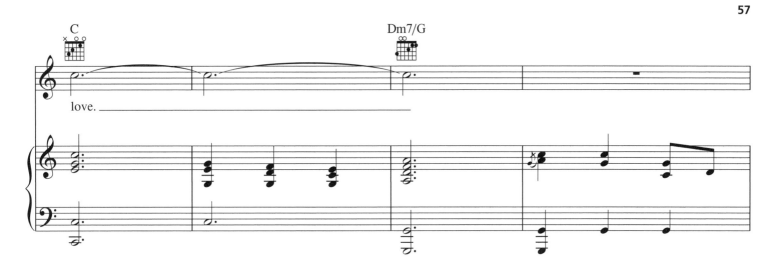

love.

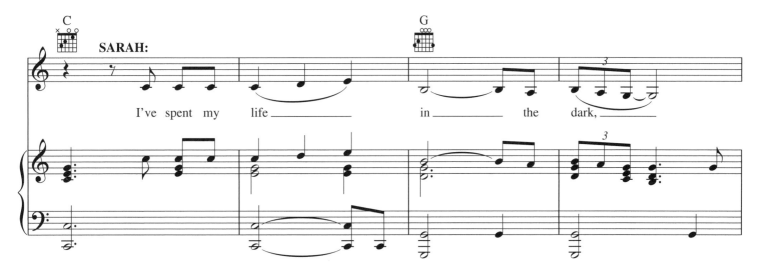

SARAH: I've spent my life _____ in _____ the dark, _____

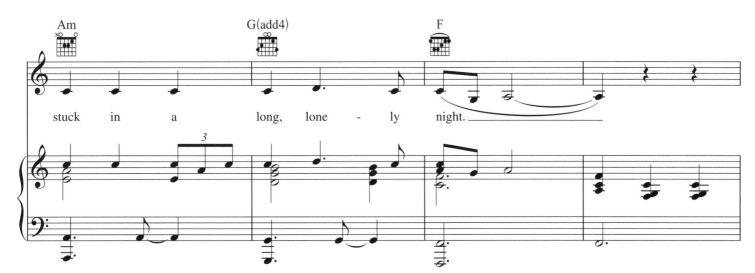

stuck in a long, lone - ly night. _____

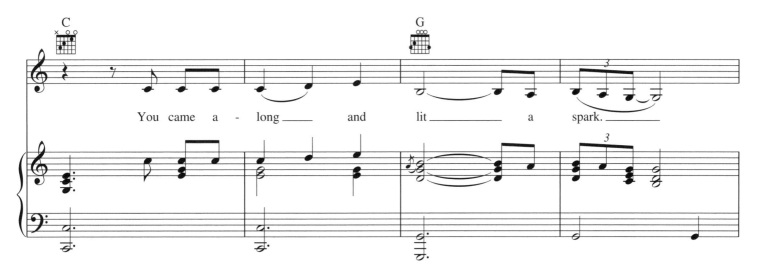

You came a - long _____ and lit _____ a spark. _____

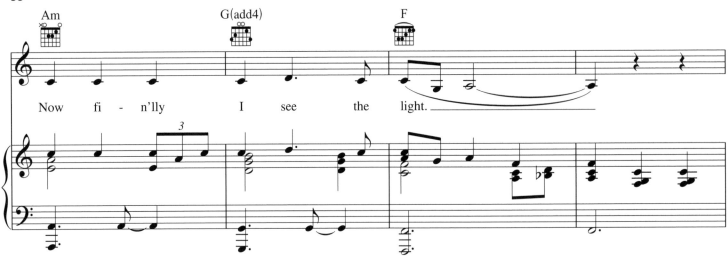

Now fi - n'lly I see the light.

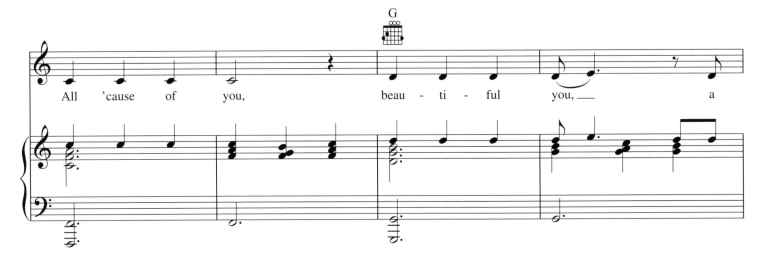

All 'cause of you, beau - ti - ful you, ___ a

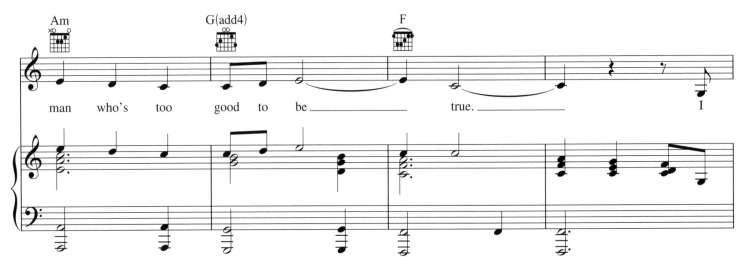

man who's too good to be ___ true. ___ I

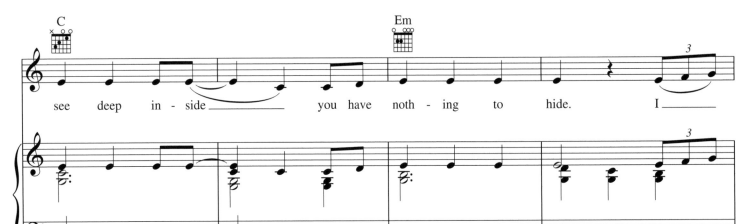

see deep in - side ___ you have noth - ing to hide. I ___

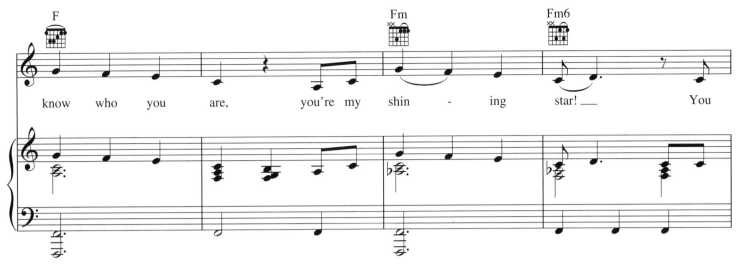

know who you are, you're my shin - ing star! _____ You

make my heart beat with _____ nu - cle - ar heat. Now _____

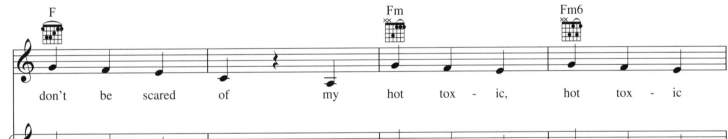

don't be scared of my hot tox - ic, hot tox - ic

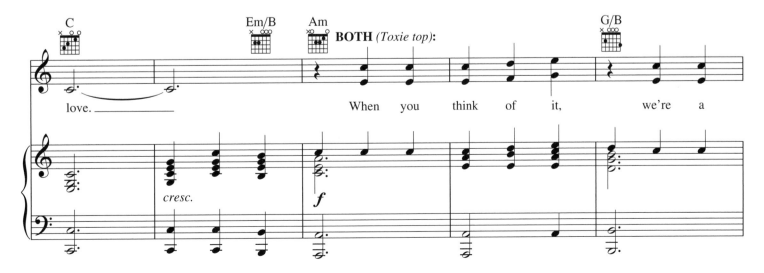

love. _____ When you think of it, we're a

me, I'm yours hon-est-ly. ___ You make me com-bust ___ with

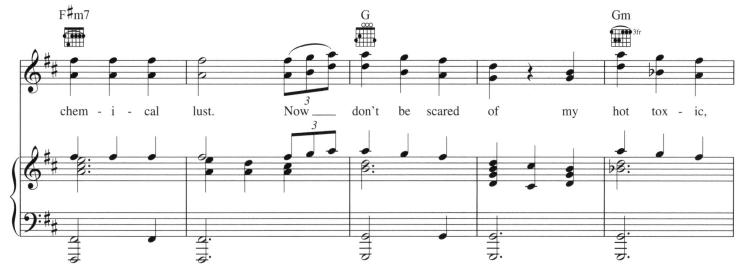

chem-i-cal lust. Now ___ don't be scared of my hot tox-ic,

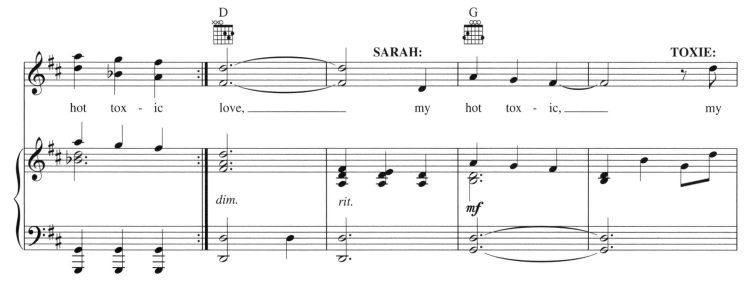

SARAH:

TOXIE:

hot tox-ic love, _____ my hot tox-ic, _____ my

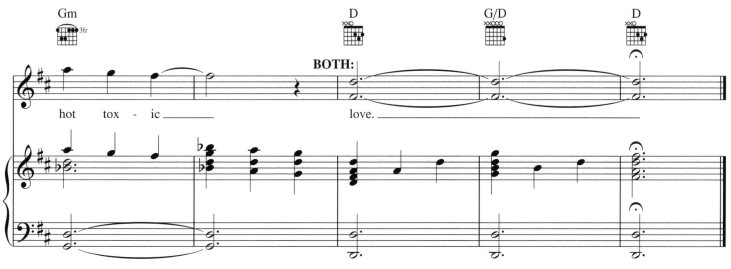

BOTH:

hot tox-ic _____ love. _____

THE LEGEND OF THE TOXIC AVENGER

Music by DAVID BRYAN
Lyrics by JOE DiPIETRO
and DAVID BRYAN

baked him home - made breads. ___ By night, he roamed the streets ___ and he
could - n't touch ___ his face ___ 'cause he's out fight - ing crime ___ and

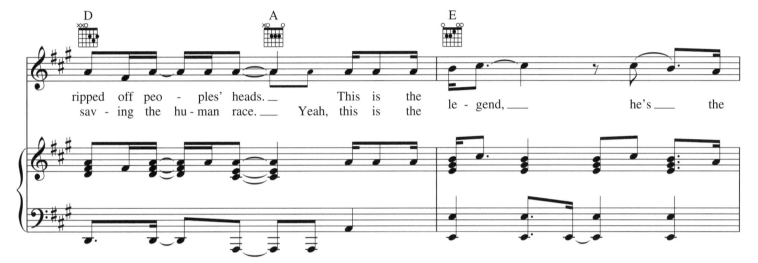

ripped off peo - ples' heads. ___ This is the le - gend, ___ he's ___ the
sav - ing the hu - man race. ___ Yeah, this is the

leg - end, the leg - end of the tox - ic a - veng - er.

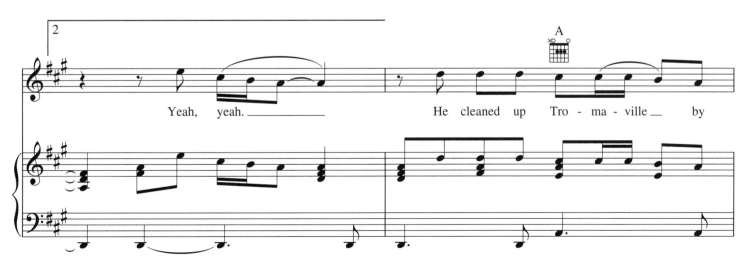

Yeah, yeah. ___ He cleaned up Tro - ma - ville ___ by

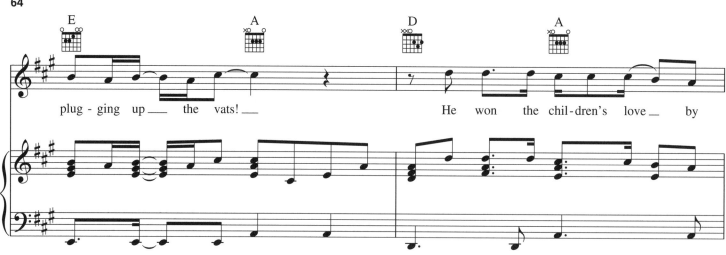

plug - ging up the vats! He won the chil-dren's love by

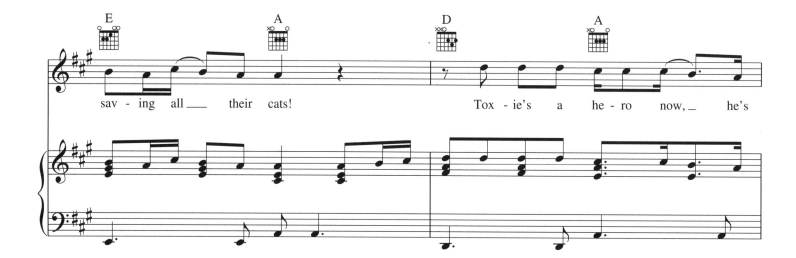

sav - ing all their cats! Tox - ie's a he - ro now, he's

big - ger than Sup - er - man! Let him lay some whip-ass on,

let him lay some whip-ass on, the man could real - ly lay some whip-ass on,

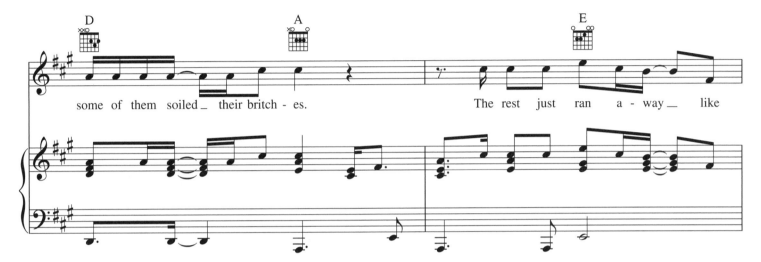

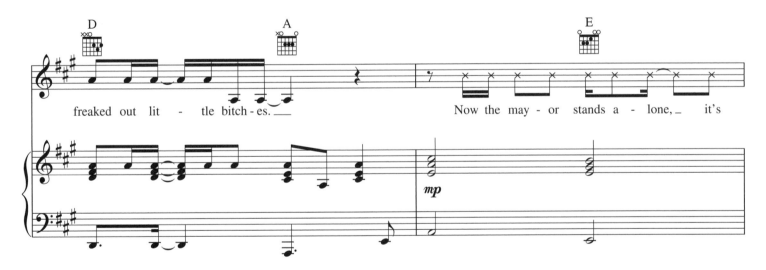

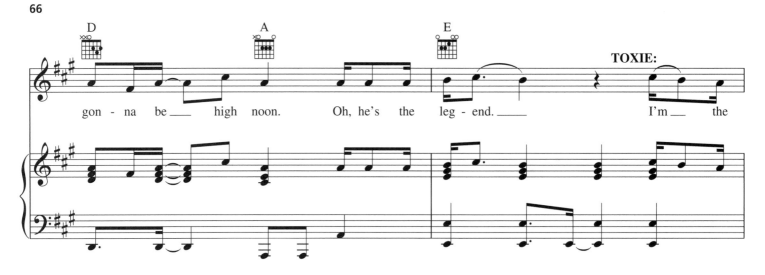

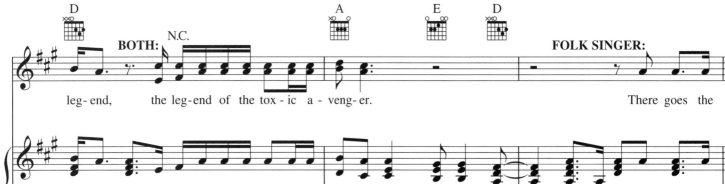

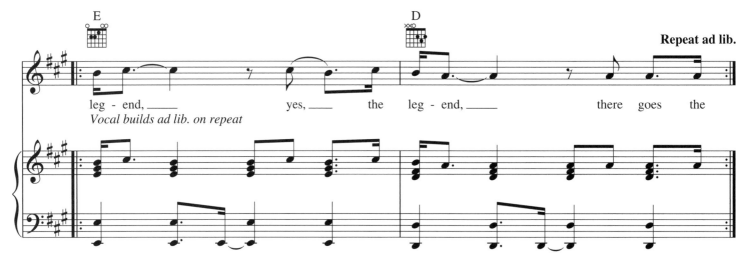

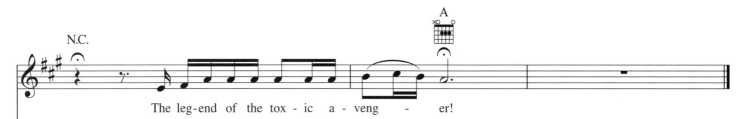

EVIL IS HOT

Music by DAVID BRYAN
Lyrics by JOE DiPIETRO
and DAVID BRYAN

Hard Rock, freely

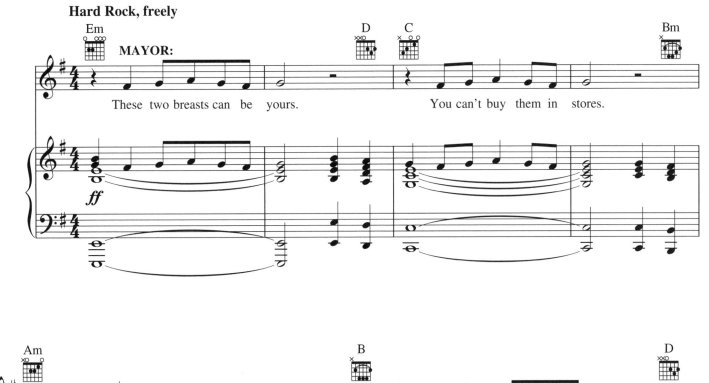

MAYOR: These two breasts can be yours. You can't buy them in stores.

Go a-head, take a bite! Just tell me, what's his kryp-to-nite? _____

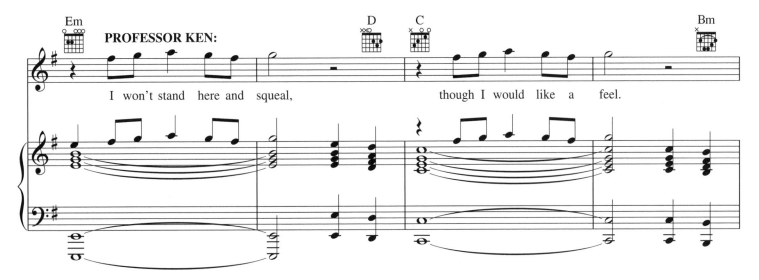

PROFESSOR KEN: I won't stand here and squeal, though I would like a feel.

BITCH/SLUT/LIAR/WHORE

Music by DAVID BRYAN
Lyrics by JOE DiPIETRO
and DAVID BRYAN

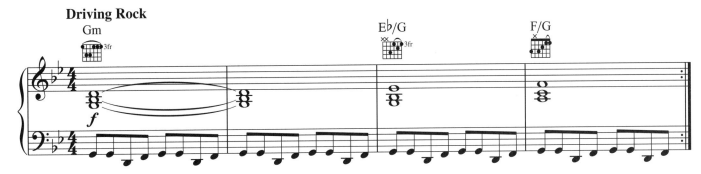

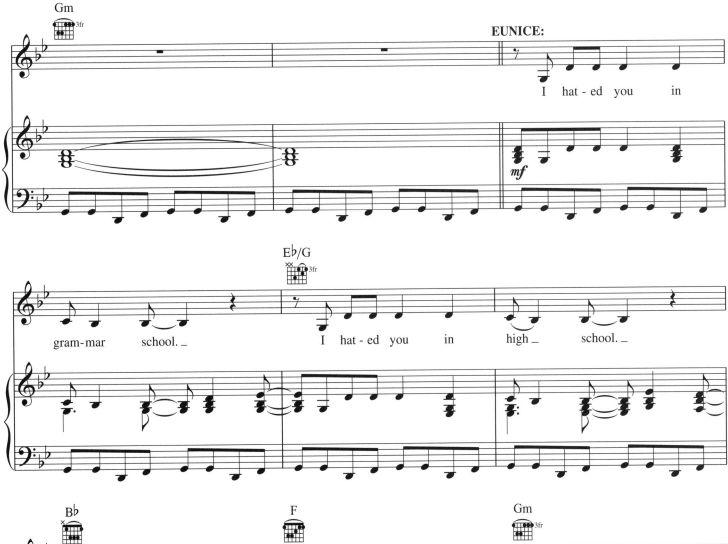

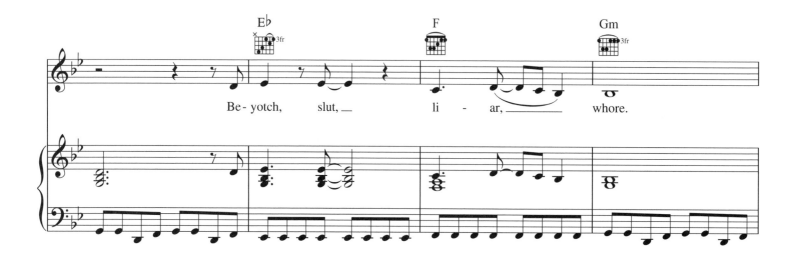

MAYOR:

Your son - ny boy will soon go bust. _

Your son - ny boy will eat my dust. _ You bet - ter tell me where's he

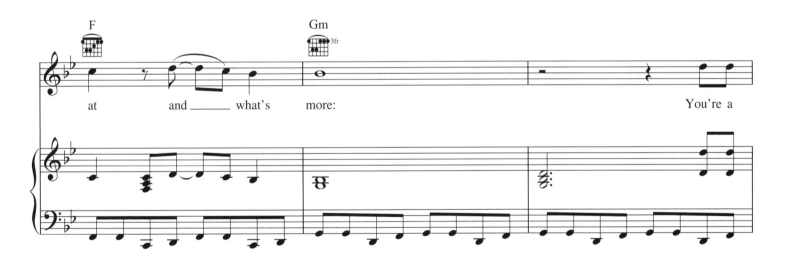

at and _ what's more: You're a

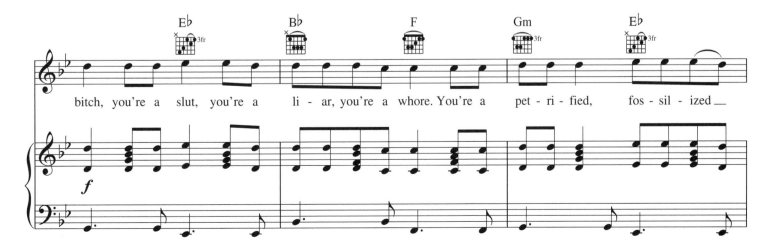

bitch, you're a slut, you're a li - ar, you're a whore. You're a pet - ri - fied, fos - sil - ized _

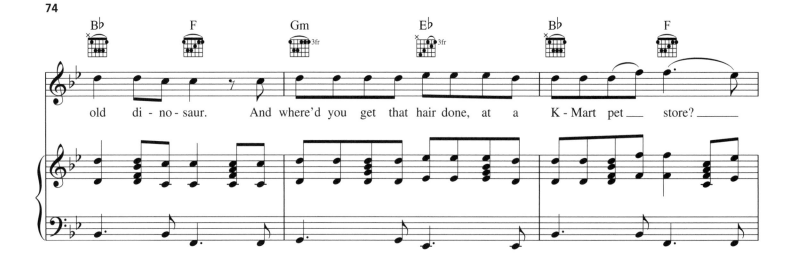

old di-no-saur. And where'd you get that hair done, at a K-Mart pet store?

Guess who won this round? Snap, snap, snap, snap, snap, snap, score.

EUNICE: *You stay away from my Melvin!*   MAYOR: *Go to hell!*   EUNICE: *Have another face-lift!*

MAYOR: *Oh no she didn't!*   EUNICE: *Oh yes she did.*   You're a bitch, you're a slut! You're a

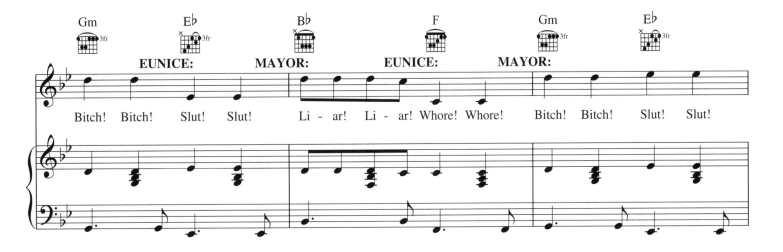

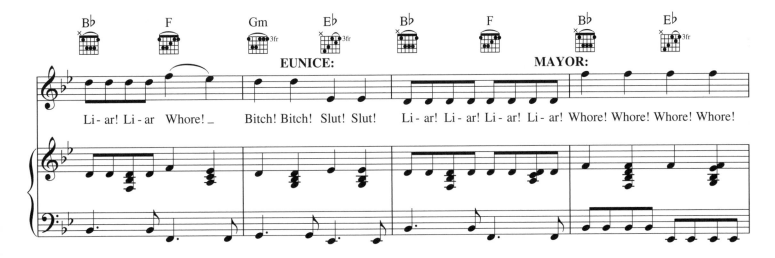

YOU TORE MY HEART OUT

Music by DAVID BRYAN
Lyrics by JOE DiPIETRO
and DAVID BRYAN

Gentle Pop Ballad

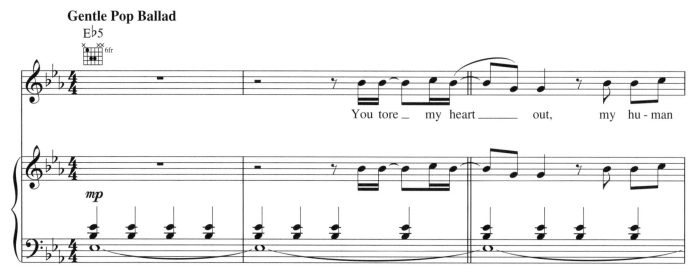

You tore __ my heart __ out, my hu - man

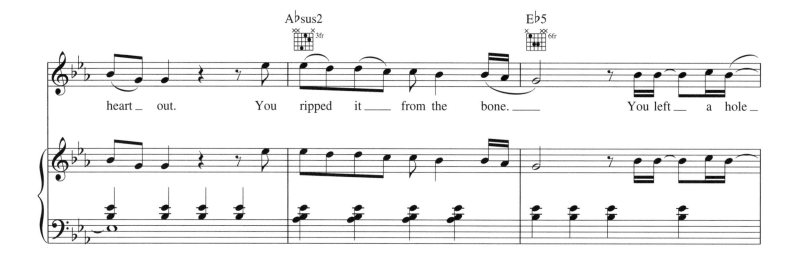

heart __ out. You ripped it __ from the bone. __ You left __ a hole __

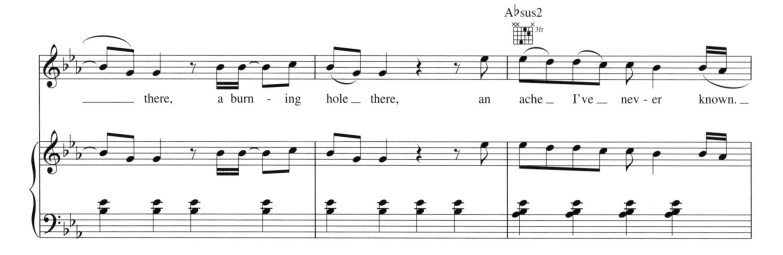

__ there, a burn - ing hole __ there, an ache __ I've __ nev - er known. __

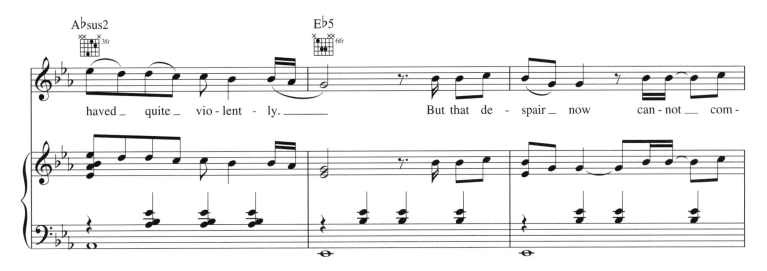

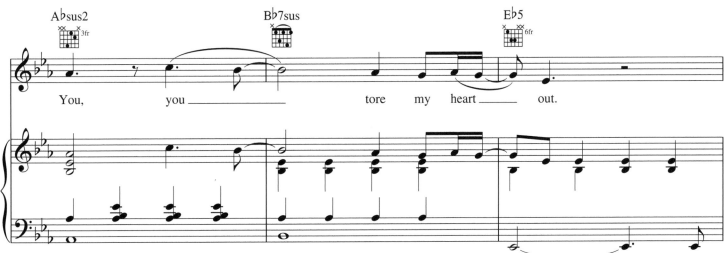

gan here, a soul __ who's __ hard to love. ____ It's kind __ of fun-

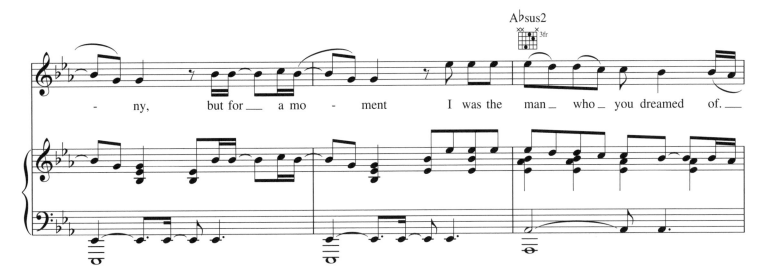

- ny, but for __ a mo - ment I was the man __ who __ you dreamed of. __

Now that dream has died. ____

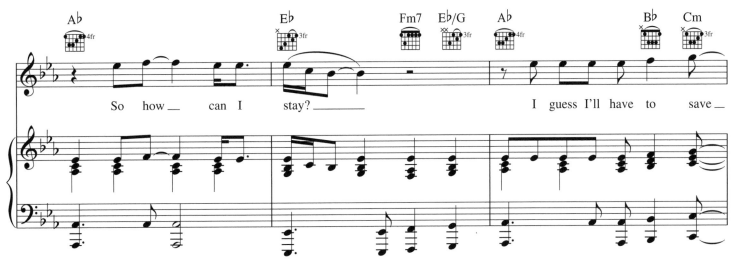

So how __ can I stay? ____ I guess I'll have to save __

ALL MEN ARE FREAKS

Music by DAVID BRYAN
Lyrics by JOE DiPIETRO
and DAVID BRYAN

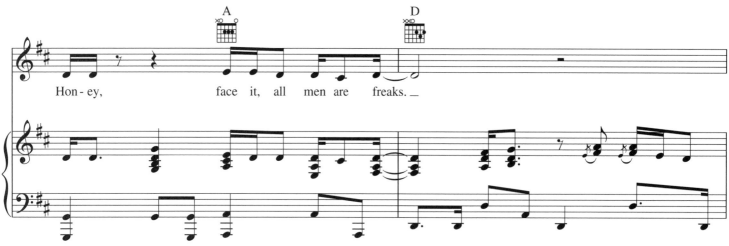

Hon - ey, face it, all men are freaks. _

Sweet - heart, face it, all men are freaks. _

SARAH:

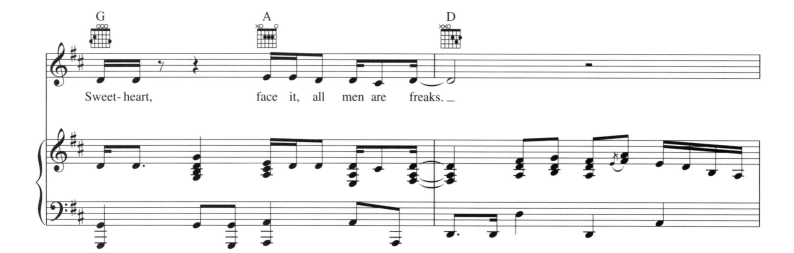

I've had my share of men be - fore, _ yeah, I've been in man - y ___ beds.

I've felt their lump - y bod - ies, girl, ___ and I've rubbed on their _ bald _ heads. _

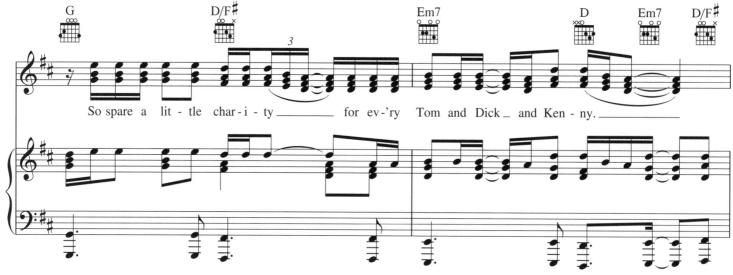

So spare a lit-tle char-i-ty _____ for ev-'ry Tom and Dick _ and Ken -ny. _____

And some-how o-ver-look the faults, _____ of which they all have

add SARAH:

man - y! _____ It's a bur-den ev-'ry wom-an shares, ___ be she

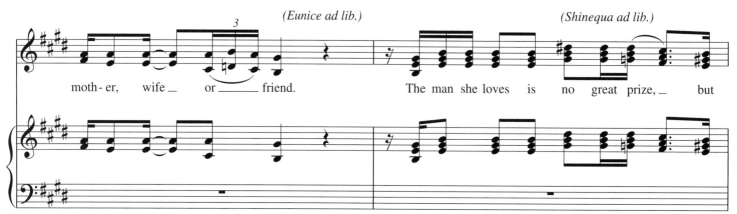

(Eunice ad lib.)   (Shinequa ad lib.)

moth- er, wife _ or _____ friend.   The man she loves is no great prize, _ but

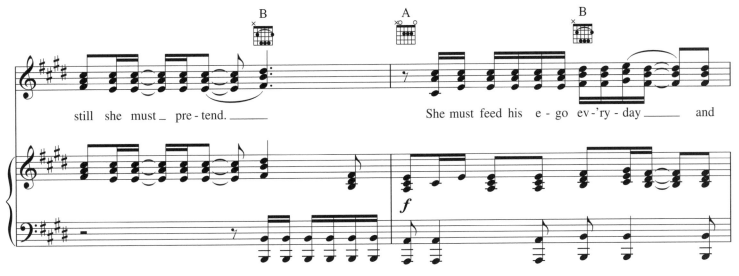

still she must _ pre - tend. _____ She must feed his e - go ev - 'ry - day _____ and

hear the bab - ble he _____ speaks. Sis - ters, let's face it, all men are freaks. _

SARAH:
I love my freak - y freak. _

SHINEQUA:
EUNICE, DIANE
& SHINEQUA:
F to the R E K S, yeah! Oh, _____ got - ta love your freak.

I would if I could on - ly see. ___

Oh, ___ go find your freak.

Go find my, find ___ my freak. Oh, ___ got - ta save my,

Oh, ___ we'll go find your freak.

oh, ___ gon - na save my, oh, ___ my beau - ti - ful freak!

rall.

(ad lib.)

A BRAND NEW DAY IN NEW JERSEY

Music by DAVID BRYAN
Lyrics by JOE DiPIETRO
and DAVID BRYAN

Bright Rock

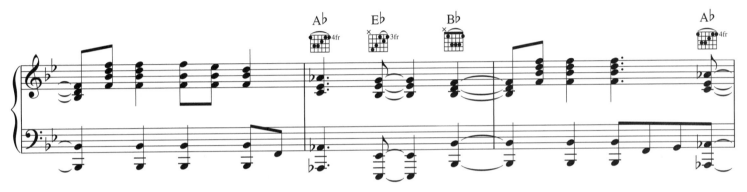

COP:

Glob-al warm-ing's

up a - head.___ The ex-perts think we'll all be dead.___ But___

they don't __ know __ we're here to fight! __

PROFESSOR KEN:

Cor - po - ra - tions are full of fiends. __

A hur - ri - cane wiped out New Or - leans. __ There's __ just one __ guy __

__ who can make things right! __

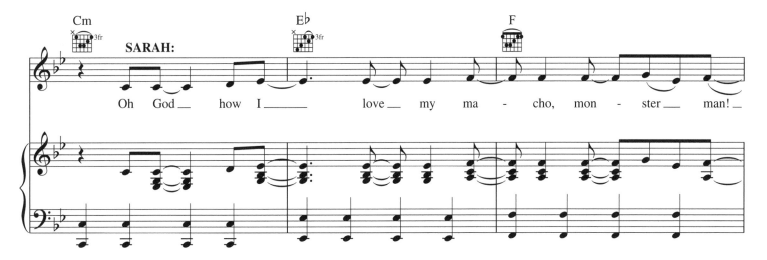

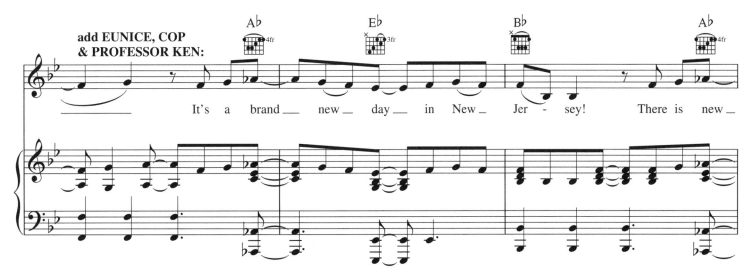

Jer - sey, so you won't __ catch can - cer and die. ____ No, you won't __

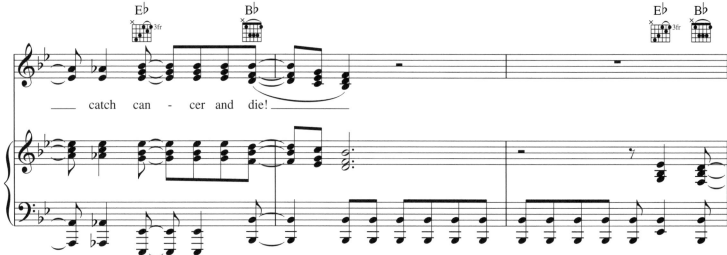

__ catch can - cer and die! _____

TOXIE:

The first bill that I plan to pass: __ Pol - lute the earth and I'll

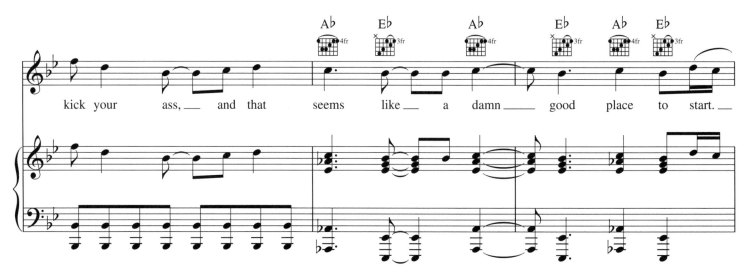

kick your ass, __ and that seems like __ a damn __ good place to start. __

EUNICE & SARAH: Oh, yeah, woo. **TOXIE:** The sec-ond thing, and this I mean: Love your broth-er, be he brown or green, or I will rip your face a-part! **EUNICE & SARAH:** Right a-part!

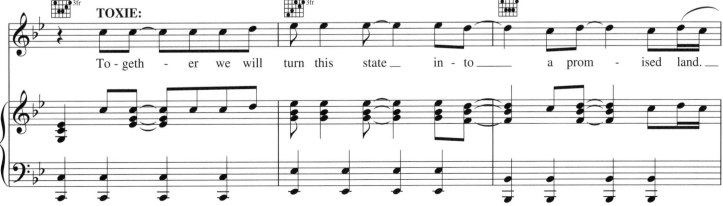

TOXIE: To-geth-er we will turn this state in-to a prom-ised land.

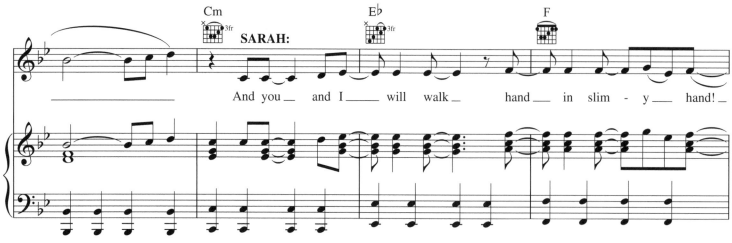

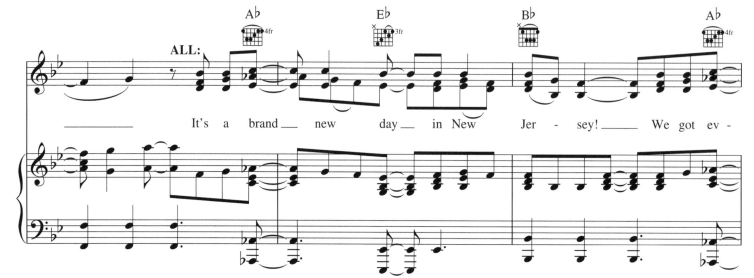

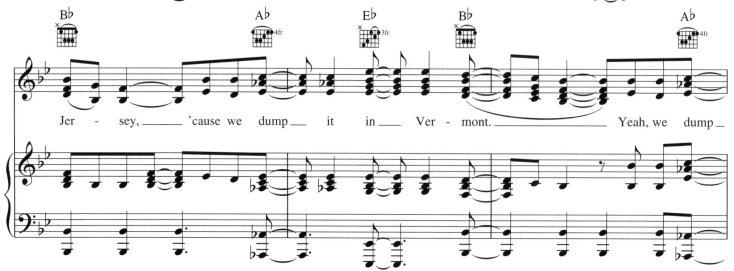

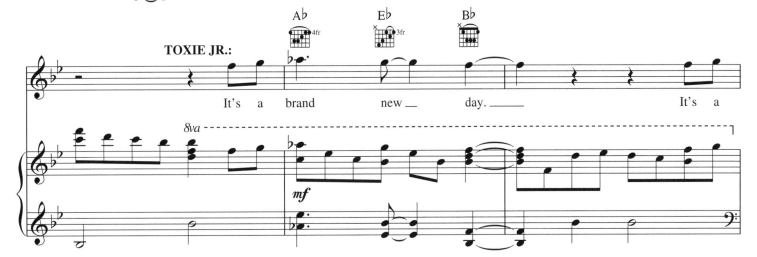

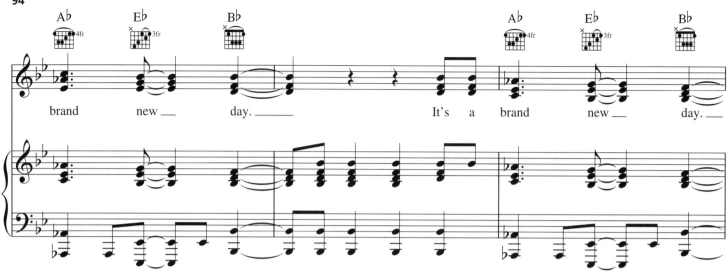

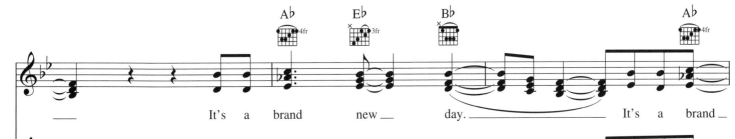

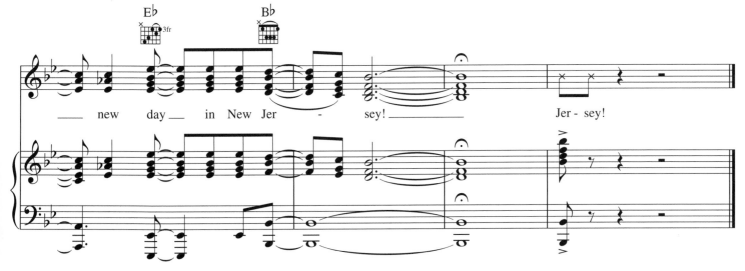